# THE MYTH

## OF

## SIR CRAWFORD

## McCULLAGH

## 1868-1948

### LEADER OF BELFAST CITY

A re-examination of his legacy and reputation

# Austin Stewart

First published in 2022 by Portmore Press
portmorepress@protonmail.com
ISBN-13: 978-1-5272-8824-9

*For*

*Jacinta,*

*Janet, Colleen, and Joe,*

*Colm, Shane, and Sarah,*

*Elise, Aimée, Beth, and Sean Augustine.*

# CONTENTS

Illustrations by kind permission of the National Library of Ireland and the City Hall, Belfast.

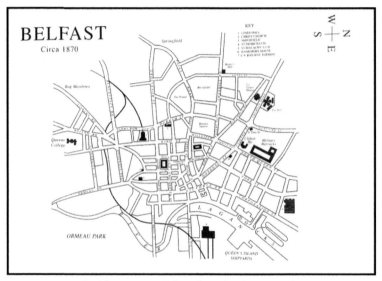

Belfast town (after Boyd) circa 1870.

# ABREVIATIONS

| | |
|---|---|
| AMAI | The Association of Municipal Authorities |
| DIB | Dictionary of Irish Biography |
| LGB | Local Government Board |
| UVF | Ulster Volunteer Force |
| UUC | Ulster Unionist Council |
| USC | Ulster Special Constabulary |
| UUP | Ulster Unionist Party |
| IPP | Irish Parliamentary Party |

# PREFACE

An assessment of Sir Crawford McCullagh's contribution to the commercial and political life of Belfast city was conceived as a paper to be delivered in the Maynooth University History Forum. As it transpired, it was not delivered in the Maynooth Forum but presented at a seminar in Queen's University, Belfast, prior to the launch of the book *Belfast 400* (ed. S. J. Connolly) in 2012.

During the early 00s, the Maynooth University Forum offered postgraduate history students and established historians a platform to present new research. Among professional historians who addressed the Forum were Donald Akenson, Andy Bielenberg, Christine Casey, Ciara Chambers, Finola Doyle-O'Neill, Tom Dunne, Bryan Fanning, Diarmuid Ferriter, Tom Kaldor, Stephen Kelly, Daire Keogh, Colm Lennon, Patrick Maume, Niall O'Ciosain. Tadgh O'Keeffe, Olwen Purdue.

Over the years, a host of postgraduates from the history department also delivered papers, and many went on to publish. They included Sean Bagnall, Rebecca Campion, Carmel Connell, Paul Connell, Liam Clare, Denis Cronin, Elizabeth Cronin, Marie Downey, Susan Durack, Geraldine English, Michael English, Rita Edwards, Rosaleen Fallon, Catherine Fleming, Caroline Gallagher, James Ganley, Mealla Gibbons, Rob Goodbody, Bríd Heslin, Karina Holton, Tom Hunt, Don Johnston, Liam Kenny, Ciarán McCabe, Eithne Massey, Rory Masterson, Ann Matthews, Ida Milne, Miriam Moffitt, Peter Mullowney, Maeve Mulryan Moloney, Brian

1

O'Dalaigh, Ciarán Reilly, Frank Sweeney, Brendan Twomey, Margaret Urwin, Barbara Walsh, Fionnuala Walsh.

Just before the pandemic of Covid-19, the Maynooth University History Forum was wound down, having served its purpose over many years. Its continued existence was in no small measure due to the support and encouragement of Professors Vincent Comerford, Raymond Gillespie, Mary Ann Lyons, and senior lecturer, Jacinta Prunty.

During the Covid-19 Lockdown, the Sir Crawford McCullagh paper was revisited and further developed. It is now the context for the present work.

# PROLOGUE

*'For historians of Northern Ireland, the lack of scholarship on anything and everything is a constant source of frustration.*

*The centenaries present us with a window of hope that public focus on Ulster and Northern Ireland might translate into published scholarship, books and articles.'*

(History Ireland, vol. 29, July/August 2021, p. 60.)

One might expect that Sir Crawford McCullagh the unionist lord mayor of Belfast city on eighteen occasions in the first half of the twentieth century, would be well remembered. At the very least, he might be considered to be a legendary figure about whom everybody "knows" something. However, Sir Crawford McCullagh is not only poorly remembered or credited with accolades of achievement, but he is someone whom his biographer claims to have been unfairly airbrushed out of history.[1]

Why McCullagh is a forgotten son in the pantheon of Belfast's municipal history remains one of the intriguing narratives of the politics in City Hall, Belfast, after the new state of Northern Ireland came into existence in 1921.

## Ulster Unionism

Since 1800, Ireland had been part of the United Kingdom, a political union of England, Wales, Scotland and Ireland.

---

[1] S. Cunningham, *Sir Crawford McCullagh* (Donaghadee, 2016), p. iv.

Supporters of the union in Ireland were quite happy with this until the Irish Parliamentary Party (hereafter IPP) in the last quarter of the nineteenth century, under their leader Charles Stewart Parnell, and later John Redmond, argued for an independent parliament in Ireland. Unionists north and south of the country were opposed to any such notion that would contemplate a legislative break from the United Kingdom.

In the late nineteenth and early twentieth century, Ulster unionism as a political force rose to prominence in opposition to the IPP. The aim of the IPP was to seek national self-determination that sought an independent parliament in Dublin to legislate for Irish interests. Ulster unionists were totally opposed to this, mainly for economic and religious reasons and a sense of identity that was based on geographical proximity to Scotland itself. Unionists in Ulster believed they shared a common British or Ulster-Scots identity. Scotland was within visual distance along a significant part of Northern Ireland's coastline, and some of the Scottish islands were only a few kilometres from the Irish mainland.

In 1905, the formation of the Ulster Unionist Council linked the Orange Order and other unionist groups together into one confederacy that reinforced Ulster unionist political beliefs.

These beliefs were bolstered by a potent economic argument for Ulster to remain in the confederation of Great Britain. The north east of Ulster was traditionally the most industrialised area of Ireland and Belfast was the economic fulcrum of an economy that interacted daily with the industrial ports of Scotland and the north of England. In contrast, the rest of Ireland, with an agrarian base, never acquired any leverage in the industrial revolution that quickened in Belfast.

The agrarian economy in the south was controlled by large landowners and poor tenant farmers who rented land from landlords. Land reform in the early twentieth century transferred land ownership from large landlords into the hands of farmers who were predominantly Catholic, and this caused the majority Protestant unionist population in the north-east to fear for their religious beliefs and practice. Unionists increasingly believed that if home rule came about, a Roman Catholic majority would legislate against Protestant interests in a Dublin-based parliament. Not without reason, unionists feared the wide-ranging political influence of the Roman Catholic Church in Irish society. For them 'Home Rule meant Rome Rule'.

In 1921, following the enactment of the Government of Ireland Act 1920, Ulster Unionists, having fought a bitter political battle against any form of home rule for Ireland, now found themselves saddled with a limited home rule parliament in Belfast that had jurisdiction over six northern counties. In this context, the political fortunes of Sir Crawford McCullagh both rose and fell.

## Crawford McCullagh in context

Crawford McCullagh was a unionist politician and a member of the Orange Order and he was a member of Belfast Corporation for 40 years (1906-46). Very early in life, he became a successful businessman in Belfast and acquired enormous wealth.

In 1911, he served as High Sheriff of Belfast and in 1915 he became the second President of the Amalgamated Municipalities of Ireland. He was knighted in 1915 and created a baronet in 1935, and both titles enabled him to be referred to as Sir Crawford McCullagh. While a knighthood could not be inherited, the baronetage was a higher title and was hereditary.

McCullagh was lord mayor of Belfast for the first time in 1914 and became the longest serving mayor or lord mayor of any municipality on the island of Ireland during the twentieth century. He was lord mayor of Belfast from 1914 to 1917, and from 1931 to 1946 (with a brief break in between), a total of eighteen years. In 1917, the British government established an all-party Irish Convention to resolve the Irish Question that had beleaguered both British and Irish politicians for generations. McCullagh, though no longer lord mayor, attended the Convention representing Belfast Corporation.

The Convention ended in failure and McCullagh returned to Belfast politics, where the unionists had a thorough and overall control, a control that spawned an apathy and ennui in the political class where 'corruption and graft flourished'.[2]

McCullagh sat in both houses of the Northern Ireland parliament. He was a member of the first House of Commons in 1921-25 and he failed to be re-elected to the second parliament in 1925. As the lord mayor of Belfast, he was an ex officio member of the Northern Ireland Senate from 1931 to 1946 and he served as Deputy Speaker of the Senate from 1939 to 1941. In the 1930s, McCullagh was

---

[2] Matthew Potter, *A history of the association of municipal authorities of Ireland 1912-2012* (Dublin, 2012), p. 122.

credited with building up and presiding over a well-organised unionist party machine in the corporation. It became known as the 'City Hall Party' and dominated council politics. The 'City Hall Party' were staunchly unionist, but the Official Unionist Party in Glengall Street saw them as a threat. In 1936, both the Official Unionist Party and the City Hall Unionist clique ran rival candidates in one Belfast District.

## Unanswered questions

Despite his high profile in Belfast politics, there are unanswered questions about McCullagh's rise to prominence. It is unclear how he got his wealth in early life that allowed him to never draw on the public purse for the entertaining and the guesting of visiting dignitaries from near and afar. He had a reputation for being the soul of generosity and freely lavished on banquets and parties. Previous high profile persons with deep pockets, like Otto Joffè, had acted as lord mayor and did not draw on the public purse in the execution of their duties, but their term of office was short. Another person who did not draw on the public purse when lord mayor was Lord Pirrie[3] but he himself ended up bankrupt.

People presumed McCullagh had made enormous money in his business dealings, but as any records of these are no longer extant, it is difficult to source a paper trail for his accumulated wealth. McCullagh loved the trappings of wealth and moved house to live in a home that did justice to his

---

[3] J. Pirrie was Chairman of the Belfast shipbuilders Harland and Wolff between 1895 and 1924. He served as Lord Mayor of Belfast in 1896 and 1897.

status as lord mayor. In this, he was not unique.[4]

A whiff of scandal and controversy around McCullagh emerged in the mid to late 1920s when he served as chairman of the Housing Committee of Belfast Corporation. In 1925, the auditor of the Northern Ireland Department of Local government discovered several irregularities in the financial affairs of the committee. The government responded by setting up a commission of enquiry to investigate matters.

The enquiry began in October 1925 and lasted four months until January 1926. The ensuing parliamentary report of the Megaw Enquiry detailed a catalogue of malpractice and mismanagement, including inadequate checking of accounts, and discrepancies in both the quality and quantity of purchased materials. There was evidence of contracts awarded without proper tendering and, most damning of all, members of the committee had financial interests in building sites purchased by the corporation.

Two officials in the council were forced to resign. McCullagh was heavily criticised, but miraculously survived. Politically, he lost his seat on the council at the next election but bounced back to get a seat in another district in the next council elections and served as the lord mayor during the whole of the 1930s.

In 1941, when McCullagh was head of affairs in the corporation, another scandal came to light exposing a catalogue of irregularities in the Whiteabbey Sanatorium (a hospital run by the Belfast Corporation). Such was the extent of the scandal that the corporation was dissolved and replaced by commissioners appointed by the Minister for

---

[4] B. Arnold, *Charles Haughey* (London, 2006), p. 94.

Local Government in the period between 1942 and 1945. When the crisis came to light, McCullagh declared himself to be on the side of the angels and was 'thoroughly pro-reform' in backing any proposals that remedied matters. In the circumstances, it was the newly appointed commissioners rather than McCullagh who oversaw reform and put matters to right. McCullagh continued as lord mayor during the commissioners' period and was still in office when the corporation was restored. He retired from public life in 1946 and died on 13 April 1948 aged 79. McCullagh served as lord mayor of Belfast eighteen times, an unrivalled record for any lord mayor. The nearest comparable period for a long-serving lord mayor of Dublin was ten years, and this was Alfred Byrne's term of office in the 1930s.

McCullagh has received scant reference and attention in the histories of Belfast, both in the twentieth and twenty-first centuries and when he appears, there is always a question mark about his contribution to both civic and political life, patently stated or subtly suggested. There was no entry for him in the much lauded *Dictionary of Irish Biography* (DIB) published in 2006. The current updated references number over 11,000 lives. The present writer drew attention to this apparent oversight, and the DIB senior researcher, Patrick Maume, spoke in agreement. Many people have been added to the *Dictionary* over the years, but not Sir Crawford McCullagh.

There is no doubt that McCullagh revelled in the ceremonial aspects of his role as lord mayor.[5] He was inscrutably affable and dignified and appeared to have no problem financing the office from his own resources rather

---

[5] Potter, p. 122.

than from the public purse. He had the reputation of being a 'Merchant Prince' in a city that was booming at the end of the nineteenth and early twentieth century. He was 'extremely hospitable' both in private and public. He hosted receptions that were attended by up to a thousand guests. In 1938, he negotiated with the Earl of Shaftsbury to acquire Belfast Castle, which incorporated 200 acres for the city of Belfast. Years later Belfast Corporation, in appreciation, commemorated his memory and that of his wife with a stained glass window on the stairway in City Hall.

## Power politics

Being a leader of the city for an amazing eighteen years was no mean achievement. In all his dealings, McCullagh appeared to be a man of few utterances. He liked to keep his own counsel and was not someone prone to publically reveal his inner thoughts. As an active member of the Freemasons, his dealings in business and politics may have lacked transparency, while today, in retrospect, his very anodyne leadership may mask a host of interpretations.

In their study of Belfast politics in 1973, Budge and O'Leary called for an explanation of McCullagh's extraordinary hold over the unionists on the city corporation for a decade and a half. They concluded that 'after an initial false start in the late 1920s, Sir Crawford McCullagh controlled the corporation through building up a highly disciplined party machine which only an extraordinary crisis such as the Whiteabbey scandal, could put out of action. Unionist councillors developed a permanent structure, the

'City Hall party', with leader, secretary, treasurer and regular meetings'.[6]

In 1982 the Belfast historian, Jonathan Bardon, in *Belfast, an illustrated history* observed that the City Hall unionist party comprised leading members of the business and political classes,[7] who were slow to be in any way proactive in restoring peace in the dramatic events of the riots in July 1935. Bardon relates how McCullagh and the corporation belatedly, and under pressure from the trade unions and the Churches, urged the citizens to 'absent themselves from all assemblages in the streets and public places'.[8] When Bardon came to write his *History of Ulster* ten years later, he made only one reference to Crawford McCullagh as the 'discredited leader of a corporation still in commission'.[9] In 2006, Bardon's essay in *Enduring City: Belfast in the twentieth century* judged that McCullagh's critics 'feared that he was turning the City Hall into his own personal fiefdom and that his clients were forming a party within a party'.[10]

During both World Wars McCullagh was lord mayor of Belfast. He was the First Citizen and the leader of the city, but his profile during the war years barely merits a mention. In the account of *Belfast and the Great War,*[11] he receives passing mention, the most significant perhaps being his close association with Otto Jaffè, a German-born wealthy Jewish

---

[6] I. Budge and C. O'Leary, *Belfast: Approach to Crisis* (London, 1973), p. 155-6.

[7] J. Bardon, *Belfast, an illustrated history* (Belfast, 1982), p. 204.

[8] Ibid., p. 229-230.

[9] J. Bardon, *A history of Ulster* (Belfast, 1992), p. 584.

[10] F. W. Boal, S. A. Royle (eds), *Enduring city: Belfast in the twentieth century* (Belfast, 2006), p.128.

[11] K. Haines, *Belfast and the Great War* (Gloucestershire, 2016).

merchant and former lord mayor (1899 and 1904). Jaffè presided over the committee that elected McCullagh as lord mayor in 1914 and 1915.

At the end of 1915 McCullagh failed to prevent the corporation declaring 'no contract shall be entered into with any person of German or Austrian nationality; or any firm or company whose subscribed capital is held or controlled by persons of German or Austrian nationality. . . any such contracts now in existence should be terminated as soon as possible'.[12] Six months later, Jaffè, under a cloud because of his German family and business connections, resigned his Alderman seat in the corporation and left Ireland for England in June 1916. With his mentor gone, McCullagh wisely did not seek re-election as lord mayor in 1917.

In his account of Belfast in the second world war, *The Blitz, Belfast in the war years,* Brian Barton assigned no leadership role to the lord mayor, other than to mention that Crawford McCullagh declared that the decline of the shipbuilding and linen industries in the inter-war years were 'brought about by problems over which neither the [Stormont] government nor the [Belfast] municipality has any control'.[13] In his definitive work *Northern Ireland in the second world war,*[14] Professor John Blake made no reference to any role or initiative pursued by the lord mayor of Belfast when the city was bombed in 1941.

Professor Alvin Jackson, referring to the financial mismanagement of the corporation in the 1920s and 1930s, identified McCullagh as the dominant power figure in the

---

[12] Haines, pp. 58-59.
[13] B. Barton, *The Blitz, Belfast in the war years* (Belfast, 1989), p. 2.
[14] J. W. Blake, *Northern Ireland in the second world war* (Belfast, HMSO, 1956).

city's politics. He concluded that McCullagh 'characterised a particular type of louche businessman in the unionist establishment of the time'.[15]

Jackson observes that a party boss of the calibre of McCullagh tempered the approach of the unionist government in broaching serious reform.[16] The 1927 report 'that urged the more rigorous monitoring of local government contracts' had outlined sweeping changes which were ignored. Not until McCullagh's time on the corporation was nearing an end did two key initiatives at the end of the war put house building on a firm basis. The first was the creation in June 1944 of a separate Ministry of Health and Local Government, and the second was the passage of the Housing Act (N.I.) in early 1945.[17]

In 2002, the Belfast City Council produced the first-ever book dedicated to 104 famous citizens of Belfast.[18] It included people from all walks of life including two lord mayors, William Pirrie (1896-7) and Otto Jaffè (1999, 1904) and Sir Edward Harland (mayor, 1885) but no mention of the longest serving lord mayor of the city, Sir Crawford McCullagh.

A former lord mayor, David Cook (lord mayor 1978) of the Unionist Alliance party, was intrigued by this and was motivated to write a sympathetic account of McCullagh as opposed to the negative vibes that historically hung over McCullagh's time on the corporation. When Cook set about writing an account of McCullagh's time in the corporation, he

[15] A. Jackson, 'Local government in Northern Ireland, 1920-73', in *County and Town: one hundred years of local government in Ireland* (ed. Mary E. Daly), p. 63.

[16] Ibid.

[17] Ibid., p. 61.

[18] J. Bradbury, *Celebrated citizens of Belfast* (Belfast, 2002).

was reminded by friends that when McCullagh opened the Belfast Zoo in 1934, the part of the Zoo named after him was, *almost inevitably*, the Reptile House.[19] He was also reminded that the major scandal of the Whiteabbey affair coming at the end of McCullagh's municipal period 'wasn't the root of the problem of McCullagh's image: it had simply been the last straw'.[20]

Cook describes McCullagh as the 'classic example of the Victorian/Edwardian self-made man' but fails to address how, having started his own business in 1893, he became the largest ratepayer in the city ten years later. Cook concludes McCullagh was never found corrupt by any inquiry into his sojourn in office. That said, McCullagh's time as lord mayor, leader of the people, mirrored an effete and inward looking leadership that was reflected in the Belfast government of the time.

Finally, the most recent account of McCullagh's stewardship on the corporation has been a sympathetic biography of the lord mayor by his great granddaughter, Susan Cunningham.[21] The inspiration for this came about when her Canadian cousin, Sheilagh McCullagh, lodged five volumes of press clippings in the Linen Hall Library, Belfast, in 2001. Her elderly cousin hoped Susan would write and publish a record of her great grandfather, a man who 'had being almost airbrushed from the history books'.[22]

The biography that emerged sixteen years later was indeed a sequential record of Sir Crawford's life. In the author's own

---

[19] D. Cook, 'Sir Crawford McCullagh, Belfast merchant prince' in *Familia* 87, 2011, p. 158.
[20] Ibid., p. 158.
[21] S. B. Cunningham, *Sir Crawford McCullagh, Belfast's Dick Whittington* (Donaghadee, 2016).
[22] Ibid., p. iv.

words, it was not an academic or analytical study of his career in politics, but it has provided a valuable profile of McCullagh's family background, the detail of which was not previously available or known. The biography skirts any in-depth analysis of McCullagh's rise to power from humble origins on the Lough Neagh shoreline to become lord mayor of Belfast eighteen times.

Drawing on an unpublished manuscript by the Ulster journalist Alfred S. Moore and an unpublished memoir by McCullagh himself and further drawing on family memorabilia Cunningham knits together a plausible biography of a man who appears in family photo albums as 'a tall, handsome, and kindly looking man'.[23] A huge drawback for the author, and for anyone coming after, was the absence of any personal papers. For reasons unknown, McCullagh's daughter-in-law burnt most of McCullagh's private and business papers so that the paper trails relating to McCullagh's political and business dealings were nonexistent. McCullagh's biographer can give no reason for what she refers to as an 'act of historical vandalism'.[24]

McCullagh's obituary in 1948 first mooted a reference to McCullagh as the Dick Whittington of Belfast, presumably with reference to a rags-to-riches story. A more satisfactory approach to contextualising McCullagh's period as lord mayor of Belfast may be to seek a comparison with the longest-serving lord mayor of Dublin, Alfie Byrne, during the 1930s. Both men came from humble backgrounds. Both men between the world wars in the early 20th century faced similar

---

[23] Ibid., p. iii.
[24] Ibid.,p. 328.

challenges in their civic role and responded according to their times and circumstances with some aplomb. Ironically, both men are little remembered today in their respective cities despite Alfie Byrne's fame for being 'the shaking hand of Dublin', and McCullagh for being the most largesse of any lord mayor in these islands and whose control of the Belfast Corporation may have been exercised with a Machiavellian flair.

Chapter 1 explores how Belfast comes of age in late Victorian times. Chapter 2 follows the ascent of Crawford McCullagh as the town becomes a city. Chapter 3 tracks the political rise of Sir Crawford McCullagh. Chapter 4 tells of civil war on the streets of Belfast as McCullagh prepares to enter parliament. Chapters 5 and 6 narrate McCullagh's role in the Northern Ireland parliament (1921-25) and Senate (1931-46).

Chapter 7 seeks parallels between the careers of the two longest serving lord mayors of Belfast and Dublin in the early twentieth century. Both men faced a housing crisis in their respective cities. McCullagh narrowly missed going to jail for his part in a housing scandal, while Alfie Byrne, as lord mayor of Dublin, and a director of the Royal Liver Friendly Society, exercised questionable leverage in having his constituents housed before others.

# 1

# AS BELFAST COMES OF AGE

*Mighty oaks from little acorns grow* - proverb

The transformation of Belfast from a town of 53,000 inhabitants in 1831 to a city of 349,000 in 1901 'marked the golden age of a British city when power was transferred from an oligarchic corporation to a new class of wealthy entrepreneurs who embarked on a massive programme of organisation and investment'.[25] Belfast was to become a mirror-image of what was happening in British cities elsewhere. In the second half of the nineteenth century, most Irish towns were depopulated, with only one in three of the country's population living in urban areas by 1901.

Belfast was different. The extent of its industrial development in the latter part of the nineteenth century put it in a different league from other urban centres. Its industrial growth mirrored the industrial growth of cities in England and, by 1911, it was the eighth largest urban centre in the British Isles. If cities could be said to possess an individual persona, Belfast's growing sense of importance was reflected in the bourgeoning magnificence of its physical fabric.

---

[25] S. J. Connolly, *Belfast: The Rise and Fall of a Civic Culture?* in O. Purdue (ed), *Belfast: The Emerging City 1850-1914* (Dublin, 2013), p. 25.

## New physical fabric

The first new initiative was the widening of Victoria Street to replace what was once a slum area. A new town hall was built there. The cattle market in Smithfield, the pork market at Waring Street, and horse fairs at York Street were all moved to new market buildings.

These initiatives improved the urban setting and over the next thirty years, the town's growing sense of civic pride was reflected in the town's physical fabric. A new railway terminus was built at York Street and the Queen's College opened in 1849, its main building designed by a renowned architect, Sir Charles Lanyon. Belfast Court House was opened in 1846 and the gaol in 1850.

In the following decades, new building fabric in Belfast underlined growing confidence and assertiveness that was reflected in edifices like the Harbour Office (1854), the Custom House (1857), and the Town Hall (1872). The Ulster Bank Building on Waring Street and the huge functional warehouses on Victoria Street were themselves architecturally iconic. In 1872, the new Town Hall opened while the Ulster Hall (1862) gave Belfast 'a first-class venue for classical music – the art form of choice of the Victorian bourgeoisie'.[26]

In literary mode, James Adair Pilson's *History of the Rise and Progress of Belfast* (1846) put down in print a detailed topographical and contemporaneous account of the town, along with a vivid description of its economic feats. A generation later, George Benn's *History of Belfast* (1877) was to analyse the town's past and produce a deep well of information and knowledge that gave sustenance to contemporaries who

---

[26] Ibid., p.37.

passionately believed that Belfast was no mean city.

In 1888, Queen Victoria conferred the status of 'city' on Belfast, and the 1891 census recorded the city as the fastest-growing urban area in Ireland. Its industrial base had now diversified – textiles had an increased profile with shipbuilding and ancillary trades, while mineral and aerated waters along with whiskey gained world recognition. No less than 40 firms were recorded showing the diversity of the linen industry, which was producing more than a hundred thousand miles of cloth by the 1880s.

Belfast was the chief centre in Britain for manufacturing machinery for the preparation and spinning of linen. Enterprising firms like Horner, Combe and Mackie made it their business to feature the most up-to-date improvements in linen processing. Robinson & Cleaver department store boasted a vast mail-order parcel service in linen goods.

The journalist and Protestant nationalist Stephen Gwynn wrote that undisputedly 'Belfast is the commercial capital of the country – not only one of the greatest manufacturing towns but also one of the greatest seaports in the United Kingdom'.[27] He observed, with some prescience, 'of all the cities and towns in Ireland, Belfast has the least interest in any history before the Act of Union [1801]. She is enormously occupied with her present . . . and what should concern all Irishmen is the future of Belfast – for with it is extrinsically bound up, for good or evil, the whole future of the Irish nation'.[28]

In their indicative map and commentary *Belfast c. 1600 to*

---

[27] S. Gwynn, *The Famous Cities of Ireland* (Dublin, 1915), p. 330.
[28] Ibid., p. 341.

*c.1900: the making of the modern city*[29] R. Gillespie and S. A. Royle commented it was during the Victorian era that 'Belfast took on its renowned role as an industrial town of international significance'. Their map uniquely locates many industrial sites comprising many of the most significant of 'over 3,500 industrial premises that feature in Belfast between 1840 and 1900 ... (where) the actual range of manufacture carried out in this teeming city was vast.[30]

The two pillar industries of shipbuilding and linen manufacture were export-led and fed back along into feeder industries such as engineering foundries, chemicals, glass making, rope works. In this era, Belfast experienced the buzz of a multitude of small factories producing foodstuffs and domestic goods. As the city expanded, the construction industry prospered.

Early in the twentieth century, a contemporary observer noted the buzz of a vibrant city and wrote about 'the 150,000 workers that surge into the streets from the linen mills and island (Dargan) at the close of the day's work. I watched tram after tram in endless throng cross the Lagan and turn down towards Camden Road to pick up the workers from the island and carry them to different parts of the city, and then to watch the men who walked, pouring up from every side street; it reminded me of starlings on a winter evening sweeping in hundreds and thousands from the country to the plantation where they had a fixed resting place for the season'.[31]

---

[29] Irish Historic Towns Atlas No. 17, RIA, *Belfast Part 11, 1840-1900* (Dublin, 2007).
[30] R. Gillespie and S. A. Royle, *Belfast c. 1600 to c. 1900: the making of the modern city* (Dublin, 2007), p. 10.
[31] H. S. Morison, *Modern Ulster its character, customs, politics, and industries* (Belfast, 1920), pp. 83-84.

In the same period, new and bigger markets arrived in the city with 'temples of Commerce such as Robinson & Cleaver'. The Town Hall, built in 1868, had now outgrown its usefulness to provide a suitable administration hub for Belfast's new status as a city in 1888. Consequently, the White Linen Hall was demolished and a new City Hall opened on its site in 1906. In a mirror move, the old parish church of 1774, St Anne's, was replaced by a new cathedral.[32]

With the impetus of a new tram network in the Victorian period, wealthy citizens moved out to the Malone and Antrim Roads. Thousands of middle-class citizens moved to semi-detached accommodation on the periphery of the expanding city. For the working class, new housing was required with the burgeoning of jobs and population. New streets and terraces were constructed to accommodate workers in conventional kitchen-houses or larger parlour-houses. Gillespie and Royle refer to the 'flood of Victorian streets' that in many instances were designated in numerical order, aka the American fashion of naming streets from 'First' to 'Seventh'.[33]

## Belfast: an American outlier

The reference to street naming in America and how Belfast momentarily adopted the practice reflects the explosive nature of Belfast's unprecedented growth.

Belfast, unlike the more staid and generational development of Dublin, had unquestionable urban, demographic, and

---

[32] R. Gillespie and S. A. Royle, *Belfast c. 1600 to c. 1900: the making of the Victorian city* (Dublin, 2007), p. 13.
[33] R. Gillespie and S. A. Royle, *Belfast c. 1600 to c. 1900: the making of the Victorian city* (Dublin, 2007), p. 12.

industrial traits that were characteristic of city development in America. Asa Briggs, in his *Victorian Cities* (London, 1963) argued that cities did not follow the same growth pattern. Some Victorian cities emerged from small and older towns, while others were amalgamations that fused into newer urban areas. Belfast was different again and more closely resembled the new cities of the United States.

The inflow of immigrants into Belfast mirrored what was happening in the great American cities. Chicago inhabitants, for instance, came from every part of the globe.[34] It was a 'shock city' of the 1890s, emerging from a struggling village sunk in the mud of a prairie creek.[35]

During the decade between 1880 and 1890, large-scale emigration pumped up the population and the US experienced its great 'urban revolution' in the late nineteenth and early twentieth century. In that decade, Chicago more than doubled its size and other cities did likewise.[36] One commentator at the time noted that the urban movement 'swells the number of classes most exposed to agitation and discontent, intensifies the dangers to be apprehended from social upheavals and widens the chasms between classes'.[37]

Belfast population exploded around the same time, quadrupling to 350,000, and while the disparate nature of the immigrants to Belfast city (unlike Chicago) was less diverse, religious differences created uncertainty and unrest. The bulk of immigrants to the city were of Catholic persuasion, and

---

[34] Asa Briggs, *Victorian Cities* (London, 1963), p. 55.
[35] Ibid., p. 56.
[36] Ibid., p. 80.
[37] Asa Briggs, *Victorian Cities* (London, 1963), quote from Henry Fletcher in *The Drift of Population to Cities* (1891), p.81.

native Protestant workers feared for their jobs as Catholics came seeking work. Sectarian animosities seemed inevitable.

Just as the impact of mass production at the time changed the way Americans dressed, shopped, and ate, similar fashions were to emerge in Belfast. The iconic Bank Buildings became a fitting temple of haberdashery and fashion.[38] Previously, it had housed the Belfast Bank and converted to a wholesale drapery firm, Robertson, Leslie, Ferguson. The floor area of the building was a massive three acres, and the firm was one of the largest stores in Ireland with 250 employees. Before the First World War, there were huge demographic changes in western society that heavily influenced the demand for commodities and services.

Urbanisation fostered an increased demand for goods and facilities. Smaller families had more disposable income to spend on themselves. As living conditions improved, a higher proportion of the population acquired home ownership and secure renting opportunities. Homes required furnishings and fittings, and the expectations of the middle classes were, over time, emulated by the working class.[39]

In the closing decades of the nineteenth century, the evolution of the distributive trades was a 'revolution'. In the retailing sector, it took many forms, not least in the clothing industry with the development of ready-made clothing and its range of specialisation and sub-division; this was linked to major social and economic changes. Rising living standards among the working class saw a demand for relatively cheap goods supplied by the multiples and co-operatives. A growing

---

[38] The Bank Buildings were gutted by fire on 28 August 2018.
[39] W. Hamish Fraser, *The Coming of the Mass Market 1850-1914* (London, 1981), p.13.

middle class sought access to a greater choice of goods and demanded better quality food. New technological advances in manufacturing, and change affecting the means of production, ushered in new retailing methods.

In the 1890s, the shopping experience in UK cities and elsewhere was transformed with the emergence of the multi-function department store. While clothes continued to be made at home by the middle and working class, the material was supplied by drapers, mercers, and haberdashers. The introduction of the sewing machine encouraged home dressmaking and, in response, shops widened the range of dressmaking materials available, creating fashion lines previously absent.

Belfast department stores rose to the challenge and developed their facilities – toilets, writing rooms, goods being delivered, and strict adherence to cash rather than credit dealings.[40] Prices were fixed and marked up, as opposed to managers and department heads estimating what the customer might pay. Profit margins were low, but the strategy was to achieve returns on large volumes of business. Escalators, lifts and restaurants were deemed more important than high prices.

Newspaper advertising grew in importance. Window and front-of-shop displays were essential to maintain reputation. Department stores aimed to outdo the conventional draper by stocking an increasing range of dresses, coats, suits, blouses, haberdashery and trimmings.[41] *Stock it and they will come* was the new retail philosophy.

---

[40] Ibid., p. 131.
[41] Ibid., p. 132.

Once inside the department store, a large staff of 'shop-walkers' was invariably on hand to direct the shopper to the area most conducive to meet his or her shopping needs. All kinds of goods could be found under the roof of the department store: carpets, paint, wallpaper, furniture, beds, tables, dishes, plates, potteries, glass, candles, paraffin and gas; pots and pans, kettles and saucepans, cutlery, soaps and soap powder. The possibilities were endless for the enterprising entrepreneur, department owner or manager.

This was the world of Crawford McCullagh in the last decade of the nineteenth century, and it was in the 'rag trade' in Belfast that he first came to prominence.

## A meteoric rise

The contemporary journalist and novelist, Frank Frankfort Moore, wrote about the wonder of Belfast – he said it had grown in the previous 70 years as few towns in the world; that it launched the largest ships the world had ever seen; and its docks repaired the biggest ships across the world. Furthermore, it had the largest rope works in existence, the largest spinning mill, and exercised world dominance in whiskey and tobacco manufacturing. The Sirocco works in the last third of the century had revolutionised the tea trade and introduced the Indian leaf to the marketplace. The commercial printing works of Messrs McCaw, Stevenson & Orr Limited invented the process of transparent printing, using the glue named *seccotine*, and other articles that were in daily use across the world.[42]

---

[42] F. Moore, *The truth about Ulster* (London, 1914), p. 278.

Moore wrote that he found Cave Hill, which overlooks Belfast, bore a resemblance to Table Mountain, which dominates Cape Town in South Africa, and that Belfast had much in common with London in the UK. On the eve of the First World War, the middle class in Belfast moved out to the suburbs into villas along the Antrim, Crumlin, Malone and Stranmillis roads. The road south to Lisburn had a comprehensive stretch of villas and gardens of well-to-do businessmen and their families.

Factory owners in the city accommodated tens of thousands of workers in houses, comprising all conveniences, within easy reach of the workplace. Moore observed that wealth was not essential to comfort in Belfast. Corporation health inspectors were so vigilant regarding food hygiene 'that food adulteration, the curse of so many industrial towns, is practically unknown'.[43]

Moore quoted statistics on city pauperism as being one of the best in the United Kingdom. Belfast had only 95 paupers per 10,000 inhabitants compared to London which had 233, while the average for the UK as a whole was 207.[44] Moore concluded that in a community of businessmen it could only be expected that utilities like the gas works, electricity works and the tramway system should be owned and organised by the city corporation, thus contributing to the reduction of city rates. The city now boasted facilities such as swimming baths, washhouses, and a fine technical institute along with a central and free public library. Public parks were plentiful, covering an area of nearly 300 acres.[45]

---

[43] Ibid., p. 284.
[44] Ibid., p. 285.
[45] Ibid., p. 286.

## Belfast self-growth

This view of Belfast buttressed the view of Samuel Smiles, the renowned Scottish author and social reformer who travelled through Ireland in 1883. He observed that 'it seems reasonable to expect that with peace, security, energy, and diligent labour of head and hand, there is really a great future for Ireland'.

In his survey, Smiles reserved his most pejorative critique for Ireland's fishing industry that failed to harvest in Irish waters in contrast to boats from Norway, and as far away as Newfoundland and Nova Scotia, that landed their catch of cured herrings, cod, ling, and hake in Irish ports. Ironically, as foreign fleets sailed through Irish waters, they habitually sailed through large shoals of the same fish that they now secured in their ship holds.[46]

Connemara, he noted, had huge potential as a tourist area, yet on his travels there he never met a single American tourist and only met one English visitor. So poor was the tourist trade in the area that the Bianconi 'long car' between Clifden and Westport was taken off the road for lack of use.[47] He considered Galway a 'declining town' and, while it had docks, there was no proper shipping. Warehouses were empty and the fisheries of the area were underdeveloped despite a century-old fishing community at the Claddagh. From the Claddagh area across the river, the mills in Galway were silent as ground corn

---

[46] S. Smiles, *Men of Invention and Industry* (London, 1884), quoting from a 'Commissioners of Irish Fisheries report', p. 207.
[47] Ibid., p. 187.

came from America and the best people were emigrating.

Belfast, in contrast, presented a different picture to the Scotsman. In this city, Smiles found the very essence of what he wrote about when he published his widely celebrated book, *Self-Help*.[48] During the last quarter of the century, his book sold 250,000 copies and was translated into many languages. However, not everyone was enamoured of the ideas found in *Self-Help*: some considered it 'a brutal book' and believed that 'Smiles was the arch-philistine, and his book the apotheosis of respectability, gigmanity, and selfish grab'.[49] Modern commentators note Smiles as 'a middle-class apostle of complete individualism',[50] 'a philistine booster who taught his readers how to accumulate capital and become Bounderbys'.[51]

McCullagh, arriving in the city 'from the provinces', represented a new class of self-made men who were full of 'ferocious and dynamic self-confidence'. In the writings of Samuel Smiles and those of others, they found an 'intellectual certainty' where the virtues of capitalism were distilled into a few simple dogmatic propositions.[52] Men, who like McCullagh came from labouring backgrounds, aspired to live up to the notions of thrift, self-help, and self-betterment and were ably assisted through temperance movements (McCullagh and his wife never touched alcohol) and

---

[48] S. Smiles, *Self-Help* (London, 1859).
[49] Quoted in Jonathon Rose, *The Intellectual Life of the British Working Classes* (London, 2002), p. 68.
[50] Alexander Tyrell, *Class Consciousness in Early Victorian Britain* in Journal of British Studies, vol. 9, issue 2, p. 21.
[51] Christopher Clausen, *How to Join the Middle Classes* in The American Scholar, 1993, p. 407.
[52] E. J. Hobsbawm, *The Age of Revolution* (London, 1962), p. 222.

Protestant endeavour. 'Homer was Samuel Smiles' for these sorts of men'.[53]

Smiles's book lauded material progress based on enterprise driven by men passionate about business and there can be little doubt that the young McCullagh espoused these ideas as he made his way in the business world of Belfast.

Smiles wrote that the idea that Ireland was poor failed to grasp the economic facts: the country's wealth had increased during the previous twenty years. By the end of 1882, Irish people had deposited in Irish Post Office Savings Banks in excess of two million pounds sterling. All counties participated, with some of the largest deposits found in the northern counties of Down, Antrim and Tyrone.

In Belfast, Smiles argued that money was abundant for all types of commerce and a vital requirement was an environment of 'perfect safety'.[54] He was not impressed with Dublin that once had a thriving shipbuilding trade, a timber trade and iron manufactures, along with steam printing, but all that was now in the doldrums.

In contrast to Dublin, Smiles discovered that in Belfast there were men of business and industry who were there to 'lead and direct'. On his itinerary, Smiles had approached Belfast from west Ulster and commented that beyond Enniskillen, in County Fermanagh, the fields were more highly cultivated and the flax plant was dominant. When he arrived at Portadown in County Armagh, the landscape boasted factories with long chimneys and, further east before Lurgan town, was a haven of bleaching greens. As he entered

---

[53] Ibid., p. 240.
[54] Smiles, p. 190.

the streets of Belfast, he wrote jubilantly that 'everybody seems to be alive'.[55]

Smiles had first visited Belfast in 1840 and now in the 1880s, he observed that Belfast merchants had a myriad business interests: shipbuilding, linen, soft drinks (aerated water), iron machinery, printing, roofing felt, ropes, stores, nails, starch. The success of these businesses was rooted in a vigorous export trade where many of the industries earned a worldwide reputation. Smiles concluded that the working classes of Belfast were thrifty. Nearly all the better working class people lived in separate dwellings, either rented or their own property. He counted ten Building Societies in Belfast, in which industrious people stored their earnings, and over time either bought or built their own houses.[56]

By now, shipbuilding in Belfast was world-renowned. Harland and Wolff's shipyards operating on Queen's Island set standards for the world to catch up. The first modern liner, the *Oceanic*, was followed by the construction of the fastest liners in the world, the *Teutonic* and the *Majestic*. Smaller yards, like the Workman Clark and Company, worked within the shadow of Harland and Wolff, while the Belfast Rope Works supplied vital cordage.

Other Belfast firms contributed rigging woodwork for ship construction. Throughout all this, the port went from strength to strength, playing host to ship-owners, brokers, exporters, importers and insurance agents. When an individual company built up a successful export market, it often encouraged others to become involved. A case in point was that of the mineral

[55] Ibid., p. 198.
[56] Ibid., p. 204-5.

water firm Cantrell & Cochrane, who successfully exported worldwide and whose success encouraged others. By the end of the 1890s, there was no less than a score of Belfast firms involved in the aerated (the Victorian term for the soft drinks business) and mineral water production.[57]

Belfast, with its newly-found city status in 1888, identified with the colonial expansion of the British Empire at the close of the century and welcomed the opening up of new export markets. Unlike the west of Ireland, the tourist trade thrived in Belfast. Visitors came from America, Australia and Europe to observe and sample Ulster hospitality at its best.

**Belfast: a Victorian tourist hub**

There were excellent eating places, restaurants and hotel accommodation to cater to all tastes. The Castle Restaurant in Queen's Arcade was one of the foremost and best restaurants in Ireland, as well as being the largest establishment of its kind in the country. It boasted a grill room, a luncheon bar, smoke rooms, a grand dining hall overlooking Donegal place – the Piccadilly of Belfast. The restaurant hosted private dining rooms and a drawing room for ladies.[58]

The Imperial Hotel in Donegal Place laid claim to being the only establishment in the city of Belfast that was renowned through the four quarters of the globe. Its location commanded a superb view of the principal thoroughfare of the city. The building rose to four storeys, had 120 bedrooms

---

[57] W. H. Crawford, *Industries of the North: One Hundred Years Ago* (Belfast, 1986), Introduction.
[58] Ibid., p. 139.

with a staff of 40 and two night porters. The hotel itself claimed it was the favourite city accommodation for visitors from Australia, America and the continent, as well as government officials and military personnel.[59]

Another splendid hostelry of political and literary note was the Royal Hotel where, in a previous time, a certain Daniel O'Connell had to make good his escape from a violent Belfast mob. By the end of the century, the Royal Hotel had hosted Charles Dickens, the parliamentarian John Bright, and the twice-elected Prime Minister of the United Kingdom, Lord John Russell, and many other political, artistic and literary people from across the world. With forty bedrooms and a staff of twenty, it considered itself to be a high-class hotel, unlike other city establishments that catered to the commercial classes.[60]

## Class warfare in Belfast

While tourism and business thrived, the view of Belfast outside the country was not always so sanguine. The Nationalist viewpoint claimed that political circles in London thought of Belfast as divided into two classes, 'well-to-do-bigots and bigoted rowdies'.[61] The Daily Mail referred to Belfast as a 'commercial cockpit where sordid little struggles are continuously in process'.[62] It is said that San Francisco in 1910 refused to name a street after Belfast because of its

[59] Ibid., p. 75.
[60] Ibid., p. 93.
[61] S. Gribbon, 'An Irish City: Belfast 1911' in *The Town in Ireland* (Belfast, 1911), p. 204.
[62] *The Daily Mail*, 16 July 1903.

association with bigotry, riots and bloodshed. Emmet Larkin referred to the Edwardian period in Belfast as 'not only a seething political volcano in these years, but more than that, a volcano spewing religious bigotry'. Paul-Dubois in 1907 described Belfast 'with its red-bricked and smoked-blackened buildings after the American pattern'. For him, Belfast had more in common with Liverpool or Glasgow than a typical Irish town.[63] Protestants outnumbered Catholics in Belfast by three to one, yet they always feared that a growing Catholic population would threaten their jobs and livelihood.

## The coming of the mass market

The impact of the mass market at the end of the century was observed in Edwardian Belfast. Belfast boasted five luxurious department stores. Four were built by local people, one of whom was Crawford McCullagh. Throughout the city, there were chain stores, like Duffin's, that operated seven downtown shops for men's wear. There were fourteen co-operative grocery branches. Tyler's had twelve shoe shops and others offered 'cheap American boots'.[64]

Cross-channel operatives included Lipton's, who serviced four grocery outlets, while the Home and Colonial maintained six stores. Frozen meat retailers from the UK had thirty branches in the city, while Scottish firms contributed distinctively to providing waterproofs and optician services. In commercial terms, Belfast city traders were not backward in extending their commercial interests in the United

---

[63] Paul-Dubois, *Contemporary Ireland* (ed. Dublin, 1911), pp. 102-103.
[64] Gribbon, p. 207.

Kingdom. The Belfast firms, Robinson & Cleaver and Anderson & McAuley maintained three shops in London and one in Brighton respectively. The soft drinks firm, Cantrell & Cochrane, traded all over the world.

Belfast port played a vital and pivotal part in making possible the trading links with the UK and elsewhere before 1914. McCullagh, as a city councillor, was to spend many years on the port board. Between 1860 and 1914, Belfast port tonnage multiplied fivefold. With its 136 acres of harbour docks and basins, Ulster exported farm produce to help feed the industrial population of the north of England. In return, Belfast imported valuable hardware and necessary agricultural machinery, along with timber and livestock feeding stuff for Ulster farms.[65] In comparative terms, the harbour receipts profile for Belfast in 1906 were five-and-a-half times that of Cork city and one-and-a-half times those of Dublin port. Truly, the commercial axis of the island of Ireland was now firmly grounded in late Victorian and Edwardian Belfast.

## The McCullaghs

Crawford McCullagh came from a typical tenant farming community. In 1858, his father, Robert McCullagh, as a result of a family inheritance profitably leased 78 acres of agricultural land on the shores of Lough Neagh at Annaghdroghal. Twelve years later, the lease expired and although the landlord was happy to renew the arrangement, he sought a rent increase.

Robert McCullagh refused to consider the rise in rent and went to court on the matter. He lost his case and went to the

---

[65] Ibid., p. 215.

High Court. Here he lost again and was given ten days to vacate the property. He did so, but not before he razed all the crops and left them on the side of the road to rot.[66] In retrospect, Robert McCullagh was probably unlucky in all this before the seismic changes in land tenure regarding Fair Rent, Free Sale, and Fixity of Tenure that became law in Gladstone's 1881 Land Act.

In 1871, the McCullagh family moved to the parish of Aghalee in Co Antrim, where they leased a property of 90 acres. Aghalee village lay on the main road between Lurgan and Antrim town, one mile from Moira and a few miles from Lough Neagh. In 1844, Samuel Lewis described the village as a 'straggling place' with 29 houses.[67] The Aghalee parish Ordnance Survey Memoir suggests that while the parishioners were quiet and industrious, all denominations were 'to a great extent lukewarm as regards devotion or religious practice'. There were five pubs in the parish and 'Temperance was very slightly advocated'.[68] There was no resident magistrate, peace or revenue police in the parish and all local disputes were decided at Crumlin petty sessions. The parish had enjoyed the name of Soldierstown from 1641 when there was a barracks that quartered two troops of horse and foot belonging to the Royal Army.

The nearby canal forged trading links between Lough Neagh basin depots (such as Coalisland) and Belfast city. Work had begun on the Lagan canal in 1759 with the financial exuberance of the Marquis of Donegal and in 1792

---

[66] Cunningham, p. 5.
[67] S. Lewis, *The Parliamentary Gazetteer of Ireland* (Dublin, 1844).
[68] Day and McWilliams (eds), *Ordnance Survey Memoirs of Ireland (Belfast, 1993)*, vol. 21, p.38.

reached Aghalee which then became the end basin for the canal. From here, merchandise was conveyed by road to a little inlet called Ellis's Gut on the south-east shore of Lough Neagh; from there, barges crossed to the south-west corner of the lough. Two years later the canal was driven through to the shore at Ellis's Gut itself, thus removing the hassle of the three-and-a-quarter mile trek by road.

Aghalee village, being an end depot, was now a key landing place in a prime waterway linking Belfast and Lough Neagh. While there were good roads and by-roads to and from the parish, carriage by the ton from Belfast to Aghalee on the canal was a distance of 24 miles and cost four shillings. To do the same trip by land was a distance of 16 miles and cost ten shillings per ton.[69]

Throughout the nineteenth century, barge and boat traffic increased on the canal between Belfast and the Lough Neagh ports. The principal goods upstream were foreign timber, herrings, salt, groceries, iron and bleaching stuff, while downstream came grain, flour, potatoes, sand, stones, firebrick and tiles.[70] Fire-clay goods and earthenware were sourced in the Coalisland area in east Tyrone, while sand and stones were conveyed downstream in large quantities for building projects in Belfast.[71]

The link with Belfast was important for the Aghalee local economy. While the land in Aghalee parish was fertile and well cultivated, there was an abundance of limestone and vast quantities were shipped on the canal down to Belfast for

[69] Ibid., p.34.
[70] S. Lewis, *The Topographical Dictionary of Ireland*, 1, (London, 18370), p.16.
[71] *Belfast Newsletter*, 6 March 1801.

building projects.[72] Many of McCullagh's neighbours in Aghalee were employed in their homes, weaving linen and cotton for the manufacturers in Belfast which was twenty-odd miles away.[73] By the 1860s, the canal had become a highly successful inland waterway, with total traffic doubling between the 1830s and the 1880s.

The McCullagh family move to Aghalee proved an outstanding success. The vibrant economy in the parish, with its canal links to Belfast, helped to lure Robert McCullagh's sons, Samuel and Crawford, to the city. McCullagh Senior had high hopes for his sons but neither of them shared their father's ambitions. Samuel was sent to Lurgan College to pursue a medical career, but he failed to enrol and instead became a trainee accountant in the city. Robert had hopes that his younger son Crawford would enter the Church like his uncle Joseph, who was then the minister of the First Presbyterian Church in Bangor, Co Down.

Crawford was sent to Bangor and, having spent some time with his uncle, he returned home clearly convinced that a career in the Church was not for him. He refused to attend Lurgan College and worked on his father's farm until Samuel, now working in Belfast as an accountant, sent him news that there were apprenticeships advertised in the drapery trade in the Bank Buildings in Belfast. Two of Crawford's uncles had been very successful in the drapery business in their time, and, bolstered by this knowledge, Crawford arrived in Belfast in 1882 to start on what would become a meteoric career.[74].

---

[72] Lewis, p.16.
[73] Ibid.
[74] Cunningham, p. 8.

# 2

# THE ASCENT OF CRAWFORD
# McCULLAGH

*'No city in Ireland (if indeed any in the United Kingdom) has so
rapidly developed itself from insignificance to vast importance as Belfast'*
(The Belfast and Ulster Directory, 1897)

Crawford McCullagh left home in the early 1880s without the
blessing of his father, who took deep umbrage at young
McCullagh deserting the family farm. To give Crawford a
head start, his older brother Samuel and his mother pooled
together their resources to pay for his apprenticeship in the
Bank Buildings in Belfast. Crawford himself supplemented
his income by selling newspapers in Castle Place (Fig.1) and
outside the Great Northern Railway Station.[75]

The Bank Buildings had a boarding house for apprentices,
and McCullagh was one of 22 who boarded there. He walked
to work every day, through Victoria Street and the central
shopping area of Donegal Place.

By then, Royal Avenue had replaced the 'old stinking and
insanitary' Hercules Street and Garfield Street. Two years into
his apprenticeship, the Home Rule crisis, simmering since the
early 1870s, came to a head and left a lasting impression on
him.

---

[75] Ibid., p.14.

1. Castle Place.

2. Donegal Place.

McCullagh was eighteen years of age at the time of the 1886 riots in Belfast and street savvy enough to keep his distance from any involvement with disturbance as he went to his workplace in the city. The experience of 1886 was to later temper his approach to violent outbreaks on the Belfast streets between 1920 and 1922, and later in 1932 and 1935 when he was lord mayor. It might then have been expected that he would play a greater role in bringing a peaceful resolution to urban violence, yet in all instances, McCullagh's instincts were to distance himself and leave peaceful resolution to others while he maintained a cursory function as lord mayor.

The defeat of Gladstone's Home Rule Bill in parliament on 2 June 1986 precipitated the riots. Protestant ship workers attacked Catholic labourers at Alexander Dock and the labourers sought refuge by jumping into the Lagan River where one of them drowned. Within seven days, civil war had swept throughout Belfast.[76] As he walked to work along the Belfast streets, McCullagh encountered wrecked shops, private dwellings and workplaces, and roads torn up with their kidney stones used as missiles.

Rev Hugh Hanna, who opposed home rule, declared that Ireland was on the brink of civil war and that a 'call to arms' to settle the Irish question was deliberated in thousands of Ulster homesteads.[77]

With the defeat of the Home Rule Bill in June 1986, a semblance of peace returned, but after the 12th July celebrations, the city erupted again. The RIC drafted in 800 constables and 1,200 troops. The riots ceased and the police reinforcements withdrew. It was a false dawn as rioting again surged in August, and by September mobs had wrecked and looted 31 public

---

[76] A. Boyd, *Holy War in Belfast* (Belfast, 1987), p.140.
[77] Ibid., p.142.

houses, 32 people had been killed and 371 injured.

The young McCullagh was appalled at the wanton destruction of churches, chapels, factories, private houses and small businesses. Local courts were inundated with compensation claims. In 1887, the government blue book ran to over 600 pages detailing the narrative of events around the riots and it resulted in the *Report of the Belfast Commissioners*. The rioting continued into late October and over four months the Commissioners 'marvelled at the intensity of feeling in the city and the extraordinary persistence of rioting'.[78] The extent of the rioting took place on the Shankill Road and the Falls Road, and significantly in the business area around Donegal Street.

McCullagh showed enterprise at work and in 1887 he had risen to become an assistant manager with an annual salary of £25 with board and lodgings included. Two years later, he sought to better his position, and he left the Bank Buildings to join John Hanna's drapery shop at 38 High Street (Fig.3).

High Street at the time was buzzing with shops that catered to the rising consumer mass market. There were furniture stores, medical premises, offices, photo studios and drapery shops. His sojourn with Hanna was short as a better opportunity arose a few doors up and he moved to John Porter's shop at 34 and 36 High Street. There, he became a buyer in the dress department.

---

[78] I. Budge and C. O'Leary, *Belfast: Approach to Crisis* (London, 1973), p.88.

3. High Street.

Such was his zeal and success that, a few months later, Porter nominated him as the general manager of the shop on his imminent retirement. His salary was now £50. He took lodgings on the Antrim Road and in 1890 he married the only daughter of the household, Mary McCully, and they then moved into a house in Stranmillis. The following year, his brother Samuel married and moved nearby.

The brothers and their wives socialised together until tragedy struck when Crawford's wife died in childbirth in 1893. More tragedy followed when Samuel died the following year, and his wife moved back to her home place in Londonderry with her son, Ernest. The effect of this on McCullagh was devastating, and he became depressed. His biographer notes he was a 'loner by nature' and, with this turmoil in his life, he withdrew into himself.[79]

---

[79] Cunningham, p.28.

The closing years of the century brought about an extraordinary change of fortune for the young man from the Lough Neagh shore. A chance meeting after his brother's death with a Belfast entrepreneur, William Gibson, on High Street one afternoon was to transform the course of McCullagh's life for the better. During their conversation, McCullagh poured out his heart to the older man and told him he was thinking of emigrating to South Africa as he was fed up and depressed by his life in Belfast. We have no record of the extent of this chance meeting other than in the following week William Gibson arrived at McCullagh's workplace and presented him with a receipt for £125 to equip a vacant shop on the corner of High Street and Bridge Street. No money changed hands other than a cavalier remark from Gibson that McCullagh could repay him at a later date.

McCullagh equipped the shop, which was located at 28 High Street, as a ladies' and gents' outfitter and he opened up in 1894. The shop proved a success and McCullagh moved to another shop at 15-17 on High Street. It was here that McCullagh employed an enterprising sales assistant, Maggie Brodie. Whether he was fully aware of her background is unclear, but it turned out that her uncle was a man of multiple means and owned a cotton manufacturing company outside Manchester. It transpired also that Maggie's father, William Brodie, from Bolton-Le-Moors, Lancashire, had been in the rag trade. Within eighteen months, McCullagh had married her and the young couple set up home in Helen's Bay, near Bangor.

The 1901 census records the McCullaghs living in the large townland of Ballygrot in Bangor parish, Co Down. He was then 32 years old and his occupation was that of a general draper. His wife was referred to as 'Maggie C' but in the 1911 census, she is 'Margaret', probably reflecting their upwardly mobile aspirations and change of fortune. McCullagh – the farmer's son – was now a city councillor and a wealthy man. His occupation had changed quite dramatically from 1901 when he was a general draper to warehouseman in 1911. He now had his hands in many pies.

By 1911, his family was complete with two daughters and a son. Both the 1901 and 1911 census records that the McCullough household had a resident cook and a nurse or nanny to help with child-rearing and domestic chores. Living in Helen's Bay, away from the city, Crawford became a prominent member of the local Presbyterian Church. He sat on the church committee that brought him into direct contact with many influential people who lived in the Helen's Bay area and who had business interests in Belfast city. McCullagh became treasurer of the church committee between 1900 and 1908.

In 1900, McCullagh's finances were so robust that he had acquired the lease on a site at 5-7 High Street and set about demolishing shops and buildings in the immediate area to build a spanking new premise with a brass shop front. Five years later, he set out to develop a brand-new enterprise.[80] Both William Gibson and his protégé McCullagh rightly gauged the economic possibilities in the expanding consumer mass market in the final decade of the century and both men entertained thoughts of developing a super-large department store in the city to cater for an explosion of tastes and availability of goods.

McCullagh was still very much in contact with his patron,

---

[80] Ibid., p.43.

Gibson, who arranged for him to travel to Canada for a three-day inspection of the largest department store in Canada, owned by the Eaton Brothers who had emigrated from Clogher in Co Antrim in 1834. In Eaton's store, McCullagh was introduced to the modern technology of the day that allowed for telephone usage on the floor of the store. He witnessed a superb use of store lighting and observed the use of pneumatic tubes that moved money on wires from department counters up to a central office. The Eaton store had an elevator installed and the floors of the building were departmentalised. McCullagh returned to Belfast full of enthusiasm and reported to Gibson, whose property on the site of the old Belfast Castle he then leased to McCullagh for re-development.

Old buildings on the site were demolished, and McCullagh began a two-phased development, the first in 1905 and the second two years later. The upper part of High Street opened into Castle Place, to where McCullagh now moved his shop. It opened its doors on 6 May 1905. The location was an ideal opening onto the junction of Castle Street, Royal Avenue, Bank Street and Donegal Place, all combining to form the pivotal commercial centre of Victorian Belfast, where all trams arrived and departed.

The rise of McCullagh in Belfast's business world mirrored the image of the city itself as a modern city. Business was booming everywhere as it became a microcosm of the emerging frontier cities of the United States. In that environment, men of enterprise succeeded well. Business ethics today is a relatively recent phenomenon, now bound by codes of conduct and enforced by teams of ethics and compliance personnel. At the end of the nineteenth century, the ethics around business tended not to be an impediment to ambitious titans of industry, and Crawford McCullagh's personality suited the times.

After the debacle of the housing scandal in the mid-1920s, McCullagh bowed out of the hurly burly of the Belfast business world, but not before he gave an insightful interview to the press. He had just retired from business when he was interviewed by a journalist from the *Daily Express*.[81]

In his opening comments, McCullagh acknowledged that he had made 'a few shillings in his time' and by self-introduction he related to the journalist the story of the little boy who interrogated his father's house guest:

*'I wanted to see you because my dad says you made yourself,' said the little boy.*

*'Yes, my boy, and I'm proud of it,' replied the house guest.*

*The boy looked at the guest earnestly for a long time and then asked: 'Yes, but why did you do it like that?'*

From this, the journalist deduced that McCullagh's sense of his worth was that of a self-made man. So he opened the interview by remarking that some self-made men do an excellent job of it and that he thought McCullagh fell into that category; he spent his life in 'producing two shillings where only one grew before'.

However, it was not the actual shillings that interested McCullagh. On further probing, the journalist discovered that what drove the businessman was the *game*, the *race*, the *chase* and the *strife* into which he threw himself with 'all the ardour

---

[81] *Daily Express*, interview with Sir Crawford McCullagh, 24 January 1931.

and freshness of a boy'. The journalist related that he sat with McCullagh one morning 'digging desperately into his personality'. McCullagh told him he had no hobbies, and that he had no interest in sport. He said that his game was his business, and it was 'the finest game in the world, huh'. You pit your brains against the other fellow and try your best to beat him and, he added with a furtive glance, 'always playing fair, of course'. To the journalist, McCullagh came across as a man focused on business who had worked night and day to achieve success. In McCullagh's own words, he was 'determined to fight the world with its own weapons and beat it ... does it not beat golf, cricket, football, heh?' McCullagh delighted in the fight rather than the spoils.

During the conversation, McCullagh's eyes flashed with a boyish enthusiasm as he spoke of the battles he had lost and won. He told his story with no vanity or bombastic assertiveness. He came across to the journalist as the most charming businessman he had ever met. He was 63 years of age and in appearance was tall, erect, and almost military in carriage. He dressed extremely smartly and was well-groomed. He was keen-eyed and alert with a fresh complexion and offered a sense of humour, but 'not enough to divert him from the major issues of life'. He had retired from business in 1928 and now travelled to Canada, the USA and elsewhere.

Though retired from business, he still kept a little office in Castle Buildings (Fig.4) as he still had 'big interests and properties to attend to' but these, he said, did not take up 'much of his time'. He spoke about his father who wanted him to follow his uncle into a Church calling but against his father's wishes he went to Belfast at fourteen. In 1893, when he was 25 years old, he started business in a small draper's shop, and then 'he leased from shop to shop, from shop to store, and from store to emporium'. And finally, lest there was any doubt about a hugely successful and eventful past, McCullagh strolled the journalist around his little office 'like a curator of an art gallery' pointing out photos of shops and stores that hung on the walls.[82]

4. Castle Buildings.

[82] Ibid.

In 1896, the old White Linen Hall had been demolished, and it was replaced with a magnificent new City Hall. In the following years, Donegal Square was extensively re-developed to match the grandeur of the recent development. New structures included the Scottish Provident, the Northern Bank, the Scottish Temperance Buildings, and the Ocean Buildings. The city was undoubtedly thriving because of the success of the shipyards, the foundries, and the linen mills. A businessman like McCullagh was on the crest of a wave amid these new developments.

In 1905 he moved his business to Castle Place and was elected to the city Corporation. He was now thirty-seven years old and his rise to eminence from lowly beginnings was remarkable and begs the question if there was a significant *grey eminence* in the person of Gibson behind his meteoric rise to prominence. Gibson was arguably the 'behind the scenes' powerful facilitator and money source that allowed McCullagh to publicly advance. If this was the case, how truly independent was McCullagh? To what extent was he the master of his own destiny? This question was to rise again in the 1920s when 'conflicts of interests' went unheeded with McCullagh's association with powerful city people in the property business when he was the chairperson of the Corporation's Housing Committee. More questionable still was the shadow that hung over him re his involvement in Gibson's last will and testament.

When William Gibson died on 1 November 1913, his nephew, Robert James Gibson, disputed his uncle's last will. He argued his uncle was not of sound mind when he made a new will in the presence of Crawford McCullagh who had travelled over to Gibson's villa in the south of France.

McCullagh was summoned to appear in court where he testified Gibson had told him he had intended to leave his fortune to the granaries of County Down to buy seed. McCullagh thought that Gibson's idea was a good one, as he had family relations 'who most probably would benefit from a small legacy'. Gibson drew up a new will and out of a gross estate of £306,601, forty-nine percent (£150,000) was to be applied in perpetuity 'to assist poor and deserving farmers, resident and holding farms in Co Down and Co Antrim by grants of money, or annuities, for the purpose of stock, seed, or implements'. It appears that McCullagh was to be the administrator of this fund and that he nominated people who would benefit from the trust. In retrospect, we have no idea how the trust was administered in practice. The judge, however, dismissed the contested case of the nephew.[83]

Over the closing years of his business career, McCullagh was the director of several businesses in the city, including Maguire and Patterson, a dry goods firm (Vespa Matches), and the Classic Cinema at Castle Place. In 1945, the record shows a letter from Maguire and Patterson to the lord mayor enclosing a cheque for £100 – a director's fee for the year ending 31 March. In the same year, a director's fee from Classic Cinemas Limited was posted to the lord mayor in the City Hall with no tax deducted.[84]

---

[83] Cunningham, p.100.
[84] P.R.O.N. I., City Hall archive, LA/7/3/A/131.

## Business interests

McCullagh owned McCullagh and Co, silk mercers, milliners and fancy drapery store, which was taken over by Styles and Mantles of Oxford Street, London, in 1927. This firm had branches all over Great Britain, and it was a lucrative move by McCullagh. The price for the takeover was never disclosed, but it was considered at the time to be a large sum. Newspapers of the day referred to the business career of McCullagh as 'one of the romances of Belfast'.[85] After his apprenticeship drapery in the early 1880s, he opened a shop in High Street in 1893 and built up a vast business.

In tandem with other powerful individuals, he bought valuable blocks of property in Castle Market and Castle Place and at one time was the largest individual ratepayer in the city.[86] In 1929, he purchased a block of extensive property in Donegal Street and York Street, at the corner of which was the site of the Metropole Hotel. When quizzed about his plans for the area and the nature of the fresh developments, he merely indicated that developments on the purchased sites would be of considerable importance and interest to the people of Belfast.[87]

When McCullagh failed to regain his seat in parliament in 1925, his biographer notes that he increased his involvement in many commercial ventures; he had enormous investments in property in Belfast, and was a director in many companies. Out of this activity, the one directorship for which he received a yearly income was his time on the board of

---

[85] *Irish Times*, 1 November 1927.
[86] F. W. Boal and S.A. Royal (eds), *Enduring City*, (Belfast, 2006), p. 128.
[87] *Irish Times*, 11 February 1929.

Maguire and Patterson, a company that manufactured matches. From 1927 until his death in 1948, McCullagh received a yearly sum of £50. [88]

In the months following the debacle of the housing scandal in 1926, McCullagh's Castle Buildings and other building enterprises were sold and, after a lifetime in the drapery trade, he retired. In February 1929, when he failed to be re-elected as a Corporation councillor, the press reported that he had bought the Metropole Hotel. Two years later, the hotel was sold as a going concern to members of a Jewish family, the Berwitz brothers, Alec and Mandy. The hotel was a prodigious property on the junction at York Street and Donegal Street, and when the brothers bought it, they entertained huge plans for its modernisation only to discover that the Corporation had proposals in hand for compulsory purchase of property in the area to ease traffic congestion.

The hotel was demolished in 1934. The brothers sued the Corporation for compensation and won their case. On the original hotel site, a modern, four-story retail building was erected. [89] It was very unclear whether the Berwitz businessmen, if fully versed on the Corporation's plans to redevelop the area, would have bought the property to keep as a popular hotel, a 'favourite haunt of sporting and theatrical personalities and journalists from the *Belfast Telegraph* and *Newsletter*'. [90] If not, there is the consideration of whether the owner(s) of the Metropole Hotel had prior knowledge of the Corporation's intentions on the compulsory purchase when the property was off-loaded and sold to the

---

[88] Cunningham, p.191.
[89] Ibid., p.195.
[90] Ibid., p.193.

Berwitz brothers in 1931. McCullagh was then in situ as the newly elected lord mayor of Belfast. If timing is everything in business, the whiff of 'insider trading' may have further fed negative perceptions regarding McCullagh's business dealings. The revelations of the Belfast housing fiasco in the late 1920s and McCullagh's role were still fresh in people's memory.

## Cinema in Belfast

McCullagh had a prominent business interest in the new leisure entertainment of cinema. In the early 1900s, a quarter of the Belfast population trouped off to the picture houses, a massive attraction to Ulster folk.[91] On 1 August 1910, there was only one cinema in the city until several Belfast businessmen saw the commercial potential of the new entertainment medium. In early 1911, there were seven new cinemas in the city and this mushroom growth continued up to the outbreak of the war in 1914, by which time there were twelve cinemas in Belfast showing a huge variety of film in plush surroundings, sporting comfortable facilities that accommodated orchestras, and tea rooms with deluxe service.

All picture houses vied with one another to offer the customer value for money. The first films were silent, but small orchestras were employed to accompany screen features, while in the smaller venues, a lone pianist would attempt to interpret the screen action. In the second decade of the twentieth century, picture houses or cinema became the popular form of entertainment for the working class. As films become more

---

[91] M. Open, *Fading Lights, Silver Screens:* A History of Belfast Cinemas (Antrim, 1985), p. vii.

urbane and classy, the middle classes were increasingly encouraged to attend. During World War I, the cinema business thrived as venues grew larger and larger[92] and Crawford McCullagh was a Belfast businessman who appreciated the commercial potential of the cinema-going population.

Early attempts at sound cinema were experienced in Belfast in 1909, but it wasn't until 20 years later with Al Jolson's *The Singing Fool* that Belfast fully embraced the sound experience.[93] McCullagh's cinema, called The Classic, was one of the first to embrace sound and by 1931 most cinemas had adapted to the new medium. In 1935, a dozen new cinemas opened within two years. By the end of the 1930s, Belfast boasted 35 cinemas with a capacity to house 28,000 people, on a par with the same number of seats per capita as London itself.[94]

In a chance visit to the Electric Cinema in York Street in 1910, McCullagh had become smitten with the idea of cinema as a potential business concern. He visited The Picturedrome months later and observed how others had capitalised on opportunities, with six cinemas opening in Belfast in quick succession. As lord mayor in December 1916, he opened the Royal Cinema in Arthur Square. The Royal was a reconstruction of the historic old Theatre Royal and was lavishly equipped. McCullagh praised its high standards, describing it as a masterpiece as far as cinema houses were concerned.

McCullagh stepped down from the mayoralty at the end of the year. In 1922, Hugh Turtle, chairman of the Belfast Savings Bank, hatched a business deal with the Ostrer

[92] Ibid., p. 4.
[93] Ibid., p. 5.
[94] Ibid., p. 196.

brothers, Mark and Isidore, and two other directors to form a company called Classic Cinemas Ltd. They invited McCullagh to join the board.

McCullagh controlled the Castle Market area, making the site available on which the new cinema was to be built. It involved the demolition of several shops and a small hotel, the Wellington Arms, and it was intended from the start that the audiences attending The Classic Cinema – built to cater for 1,800 patrons[95] – would experience something extra special.

On the opening night in December 1923, a thirty-piece orchestra in full evening dress entertained the audience, and, later in the decade, a state-of-the-art Wurlitzer theatre organ was installed while the seats were wired for 'hard-of-hearing' patrons. In 1929, the Ostrer brothers established full control of the cinema and restructured the management board, while the Belfast Savings Bank chairman, Hugh Turtle, remained as a director along with McCullagh. Such was the success of The Classic that there followed a boom in the cinema industry with the opening of The Castle, The Astoria, The Ambassador and The Strand cinemas.

Capital investment in cinemas was a significant input into the local economy. The cinema trade in Belfast was closely allied to London-based and the US distributors which supplied films throughout Northern Ireland. Most cinemas were locally owned and a growing number were linked to British cinema chains, such as ABPC.[96] Films made about Ulster in the 1930s portrayed a rural image and it was not until World War II that the cinematic image of 'industrial

---

95 Open, p. 31.
96 J. Hill, *Cinema in Northern Ireland* (London, 2006), p. 77.

Ulster' emerged.[97]

## Moral dilemma

In the mid-1930s, high-minded citizens became concerned that cinema might play havoc with ordinary people's religious sensibilities and the Corporation was called upon to act. When the horror film *Frankenstein* opened at McCullagh's Classic Cinema on 19 April 1932, it immediately caused controversy and outcry, with complaints to the Corporation. The following day, a five-man delegation from the Corporation (dubbed the 'Police Committee') received a special screening and considered that the film should be banned because it was both 'blasphemous and unedifying'.[98] The film portrayed a scientist creating human life, tantamount to emulating God which was blasphemous. There were huge protests at the idea of a ban, and a second private screening was arranged which more city councillors attended, along with Government members and members of the Senate, to pass judgement on the ban.

The Stormont Member of Parliament, Harry Midgley, was opposed to the ban, arguing that the Church had exercised undue influence on the 'Police Committee'. However, Belfast Corporation upheld it. The huge irony was that the lord mayor, Sir Crawford McCullagh, a director of the Classic Cinema 'was powerless to stop the decision of one of the committees over which he presided.' The film was shown in other parts of Northern Ireland to huge audiences with subsequent

---

[97] Ibid., p. 46.
[98] *Northern Whig*, 21 April 1932.

momentous sales for Mary Shelly's novel on which it was based. Buoyed up with their success on the matter, the Church demanded a ban on cinemas opening on a Sunday if they were in close proximity to a church. The result was that the Corporation refused permission for several cinemas to open on the Sabbath, and no new cinema could be built within 120 yards of any place of worship.

The Classic Cinema again became embroiled in more controversy with the film *The Green Pastures* (1936) which endeavoured to show how 'negroes in the Deep South visualised God and Heaven in terms of people and things they knew in their everyday life'. The Church responded that 'any representation of Almighty God shown on the film screen would be repugnant to the religious convictions of the majority of our people'. The Church, through its own film committee, called upon the Minister of Home Affairs and the Belfast Corporation 'Police Committee' 'to prohibit the exhibition of any such film in the cinemas of Belfast and Northern Ireland'.[99]

A full meeting of the Corporation debated the matter and this time they ignored the Church protest because, for years, parts of Ireland had suffered 'for being priest-ridden'. Ireland was now in danger of becoming 'clerical-ridden' if succumbing to the noise from the Church film committee. A torrent of letters to the press followed, clarifying that whatever the merits of a ban on how films in the United States showed people of colour visualising their God, a portrayal of God as a black man drew the most indignation.[100]

---

[99] *Irish News*, 5 December 1936.
[100] Hill, p. 61.

The concern around censorship wasn't unique to Belfast. Dublin, too, had its concerns in the 1930s. Alfie Byrne, Lord Mayor of Dublin, was a staunch believer in the censorship of films, books and plays. He wanted Dublin Corporation to ban the Deborah Kerr film, *Black Narcissus,* a classic in its own right, on the plea that it caused 'pain and upset to many citizens'.[101] He supported the Censorship Bill in 1928 and took his cue from the letters of constituents who feared their morals threatened by the arts. Byrne issued a warning that he was going to call together the owners of the various theatres and warn them they must be more careful about which plays they brought before the audiences of Dublin. The *Irish Press* backed him: 'all those connected with the stage should be eager to resist the degradation of an honourable profession by these appeals to the lowest tastes and desires'.[102]

Despite his concerns about the people's morals, Byrne had already attempted to open a cinema of his own. As lord mayor, he opened cinemas in Dublin on St Stephen's Green and in the suburbs of Drumcondra, Fairview and Rialto. By the 1950s, Dublin boasted more cinema seats per head of population than any other city in Europe. Byrne also found fault with the jazz movement and once allegedly proclaimed that 'the citizens of Dublin are not following the dances of negroes'.[103]

---

[101] *Cork Examiner,* 29 August 1947.
[102] *Irish Press,* 20 November 1934. 1934.
[103] Quoted in *Alfie Byrne* (Dublin, 2017), p. 95.

# 3

# EARLY POLITICS

*Public life is regarded as the crown of a career, and to young men it is
the worthiest ambition.*

John Buchan

*I've always sort of thought that politics was a high and noble
calling and a good thing to do.*

Boris Johnson

## New direction

When a Conservative and Unionist Government were
returned to power in 1895, the threat of home rule for
Ireland was no longer a major concern for Unionists.
However, in 1903, the Under-Secretary for Ireland, Antony
MacDonnell, encouraged by the success of the Wyndham
Land Act, called for the setting up of a devolved government
in Ireland. Unionists in the south of the country, led by Earl
Dunraven, were supportive of such an initiative while
northern Unionists were opposed to the whole idea.

The proposal was published by the Irish Reform
Association and Sir Antony MacDonnell was the architect of
the scheme. He alleged he was acting with the tacit approval
of the Chief Secretary for Ireland, George Wyndham. When
Unionist pandemonium followed the publishing of the
proposal, Wyndham denied he had given tacit consent and

blamed his Under Secretary for the initiative. The whole matter led to the resignation of George Wyndham himself as Ireland's Chief Secretary.

Historians label the proposals for a devolved government as the Devolution Crisis of 1904-5, and it surely galvanised the Unionists in the north of the country to 'gird their loins' in the face of the home rule threat. In October 1904, a Unionist conference in Belfast condemned the proposed scheme and called for the setting up of an Ulster Unionist Association.[104] As a consequence of this, an Ulster Unionist Council was formed in December 1904 calling for a 'consistent and continuous political action' to resist devolution and resolving that the Ulster Council would align all local unionist associations in the province.

The Council had its first meeting in March 1905. Its declared aim was to be the medium for expressing Ulster Unionist opinion, and its chief function was to work for the maintenance of the constitutional position of Ulster as an integral part of the United Kingdom.[105]

The Council comprised up to 200 members, 100 of whom were nominated by local unionist associations, 50 by the Orange Order, and up to 50 influential unionists were co-opted. Further progress was made in 1907 when the Council organised the Joint Committee of Unionist Associations of Ireland. In 1910, Edward Carson became the leader. The Council had a full-time staff and Richard Dawson Bates acted as secretary from 1906 to 1921 before becoming a senior minister in the Northern Ireland parliament after partition.

---

[104] *Belfast News Letter,* 24 October 1904.
[105] J. F. Harbinson, *The Ulster Unionist Party, 1882-1973* (Belfast, 1973), p. 79.

Up to this, Crawford McCullagh had steered clear of politics and focused on his business affairs but now, in 1905, there were promptings for him to step up to the plate and he was unopposed when he stood for election in the Cromac district of the Corporation. He was elected and was one of the first members of the newly founded Unionist Council. As circumstances around the dilemma of home rule changed and gathered pace, the membership numbers of the Ulster Unionist Council expanded to 370. In preparations to oppose the third Home Rule Bill, the Council organised the Ulster Solemn League and Covenant for 28 September 1912, when loyalists gathered in their thousands to vow to resist home rule. Edward Carson led the signing ceremony in the City Hall with Crawford McCullagh present. Within days, the Covenant had collected 218,206 signatories. No women signed because they were not invited, but 228,991 women signed a declaration promising support for the men who opposed home rule.[106]

While opposed to home rule, not all loyalists, unionists, or Protestants in Ulster were in favour of the Covenant idea. Many disapproved of the extreme unionist rhetoric that was expressed in the Covenant and about a quarter of northern Protestants refused to sign it.[107]

After the signing of the Covenant, the Ulster Unionist Council formed the Ulster Volunteer Force (UVF) in January 1913. In September 1913, it appointed a 'Provisional Government' for Ulster, and in April 1914, was responsible

---

[106] D.J. Hickey & J.E. Doherty, *A new dictionary of Irish History from 1800* (Dublin, 2005), p. 484.
[107] A.R. Homes, E.F. Biagini, *Protestants* in E.F. Biagini and M. Daly (eds), *The Cambridge Social History of Modern Ireland* (Cambridge, 1917), p. 100.

for the Larne gun-running episode. The Council reluctantly accepted the Government of Ireland Act (1920) but it played a leading role in the creation of the state of Northern Ireland and had a decisive say in the formation of all subsequent governments. The governing body of the Council was the Ulster Unionist Party (UUP) and the Unionist members of parliament for the northern constituencies were members of the Council's Standing Committee.[108]

## The High Sheriff

In former times, the office of high sheriff carried with it huge power as the sheriff handled law and order in the county and frequently this power was abused and often controversial in how it was exercised. Following the Local Government Act (1898), a sheriff was appointed to the city of Belfast who was to be the monarch's man in the city. In 1911, McCullagh was elected high sheriff for Belfast. His duties included attending civic functions hosted by the lord mayor and undertaking specific functions on behalf of the Council and providing general support to the lord mayor. It was a good apprenticeship for McCullagh as three years later he was elected lord mayor of Belfast and re-elected by his peers in 1915 and 1916. His biographer alluded to the one requirement for the office of lord mayor that was never mentioned: that of having the personal financial resources to meet all the corporate entertainment that the position demanded. Unlike the Dublin lord mayor, the Belfast lord mayor had no corporate slush fund to draw on. Being a

[108] D.J. Hickey & J.E. Doherty, p. 485.

successful city businessman, McCullagh ticked all the boxes and, to boot, was considered 'obliging, civil and polite' with a working knowledge of the city Corporation.[109]

As World War II approached, McCullagh had a high profile in the Belfast business community and throughout the war years his business interests continued to thrive. In May 1916, he bought Castle Market and Castle Lane with the aim of redeveloping the site, doing away with the markets area. The development was initially delayed because of the scarcity of steel due to the war, while the local press pointedly reflected that the anticipated development would see 'a very interesting part of old Belfast' entirely vanish.

As well as playing a prominent role in the running of his department store in Castle Place, McCullagh fully appreciated the power of networking; he was president of the Belfast Industrial Association and acted as chairperson to the Linen Merchant Association, the Belfast and Northern Ireland Grocers' Association Ltd, and the Belfast Chamber of Trades. He had his finger in many pies and, in 1915, he became the second president of the Municipal Authorities of Ireland.[110]

Robert Heron, the Town Clerk of the Urban District Council of Blackrock, Co Dublin, was the prime mover in establishing the Association of Municipal Authorities of Ireland (AMAI). It was to be a non-political forum for the concerns of municipalities throughout the country. Lorcan Sherlock was elected the first president of the Association in 1912 at a conference to which 55 of the 124 municipalities sent delegates. At their May meeting in 1914, the new lord

---

[109] Cunningham, p.90.
[110] Ibid., p.94.

mayor of Belfast was co-opted as an executive member of AMAI. At the same meeting, it was agreed to send a deputation to London to see the Chancellor of the Exchequer and the delegation met with the leaders of the Irish Parliamentary Party regarding state aid for housing. McCullagh was a prominent member of the delegation.

From the minutes of the AMAI executive committee, McCullagh appears to have played very little part in the affairs of the association. Between May 1915 and 1920, the AMAI minutes record McCullagh as attending only once, at a special housing committee meeting in February 1919. A substantial number of delegates attended this meeting to draw up a memorandum to present to the Chief Secretary on the matter of housing.[111] In 1915, McCullagh was elected the second president of the Association and the fifth annual conference was held on 26 and 27 September 1916 in the City Hall, Belfast. Despite the aftermath of the Dublin Rising at Easter in 1916, the conference focused on practical and non-political concerns – the need to reduce municipal spending arising because of the war, the need for social housing, income tax, the harnessing of water power for industrial and municipal purposes, and the challenge of the spread of tuberculosis and other health issues.

On the eve of the passing of the Home Rule Bill in 1914, the War Office in London was concerned that there might be street trouble in Belfast so they despatched Major General Macready, a veteran of the Boer War, to Belfast to act as a commanding officer for the Belfast area. His briefing extended to the supervision of the police in the event of

---

[111] AMAI Minutes, 24 February 1919.

trouble when home rule was passed in parliament. The lord mayor took exception to the role of the new envoy and rejected the War Office usurpation of his authority that allowed Macready to call upon the police and army to contain social unrest in the normal course of events.

The War Office backed away and conceded that if the lord mayor was 'so damned foolish' to take responsibility for any untoward unrest in the city, let it be on his shoulders. As it transpired, there was no commotion on the Belfast streets on the passing of the Home Rule Bill. An amended Home Rule Bill was passed on 14 July 1914, and King George V called an all-party conference for 21 July at Buckingham Palace.

The conference was an attempt by the Prime Minister, Herbert Asquith, to defuse the deepening crisis and to offset the real possibility of civil war in Ireland. The talks lasted four consecutive days and centred on the possibility of carving out an area in Ulster that would be excluded from the operation of home rule.

No agreement in principle or detail could be reached, and the conference collapsed. Unionist threats to set up a provisional government in Belfast if home rule was implemented were real, while the nationalists made it known that in that scenario, they too would follow suit with their provisional government in Dublin. Civil strife in Ireland over the whole matter was only averted when England went to war with Germany.

On 7 August 1914, McCullagh chaired a meeting in the City Hall with community leaders who represented the civic, commercial, and professional interests in the city.[112] They

---

[112] Cunningham, p. 102.

agreed to establish a fund that would assist the families of those who signed up to the armed forces. Recruiting began on 4 September and an Ulster Division was formed, sourcing manpower from the Ulster Volunteer Force.

As the clouds of war darkened and the lord mayor's opposition to General Macready's appointment became known, the authorities appointed him Recruitment Officer for the Northern Division in Ulster in the autumn of 1915.[113] In May 1915, 12,000 men were recruited and trained, setting off for the war under the banner of the 36th (Ulster) Division.

The lord mayor called on business concerns in the city to encourage men to join the armed forces with the promise that their jobs would be still there when they returned from the war. Consequent to this, the Corporation released 800 employees for the war effort. In January 1916, compulsory service was introduced in Great Britain, but Ireland was exempt as it was considered too controversial an initiative to implement.

However, the war effort was well served in Belfast by the men in the shipyards and the women in the munitions factories. The organisation and production of food in Belfast was significantly helped by the allotment movement in the city. Eight hundred plots were in use by the close of 1915. Produce of £10,000 was grown locally and the 'home grown' competition kept down the price of stable vegetables and avoided food shortages. A typical plot could produce more than £10 worth of food a year.[114] In early 1915, McCullagh was re-elected as lord mayor for the second time.

---

[113] Ibid., p.92.
[114] P. Yeates, *A City in Wartime: Dublin 1914-1918* (Dublin, 2011), p. 182.

## The women's war effort

Women played a significant role working in the munitions factories and farming the land. In Belfast, workers produced 75 million artillery shells in the factories of Mackies, Davidson's and Company, and the Falls Foundry. Women whose work prospects were previously confined to household service now found themselves with options and increasing opportunities for work in mills that produced sheets, bandages, stretchers, airplane fabrics and tents.

As Belfast's First Lady, Margaret McCullagh, with encouragement from her husband, played her part in the war effort. She was involved in raising local funds to help families in distress and acted as chairperson on many committees 'with a kindly disposition . . . with a simple modesty and natural grace . . . and was seen as a friend of all grades of society'.[115] With Crawford McCullagh, she organised the Prince of Wales National Relief Fund, which raised £50,000; she raised £14,000 for the Ulster Volunteer Force Hospital Fund that provided 266 beds; she helped raise £10,000 to build and equip ambulances for the war front; and she helped raise funds for The Rotary Club and Red Cross Societies.

Amid all this fundraising, she was closely associated with McCullagh in building up his drapery empire. It was no surprise in May 1915 when McCullagh was honoured with a knighthood at the Ulster Hall in Bedford Street for the 'exceedingly great part Belfast was taking in the struggle for national existence'. Margaret was similarly honoured when, in

---

[115] Cunningham, p.110.

March 1919, she received a CBE (Commander of the Order of the British Empire) for services contributed during the war.

## Previous lord mayors

McCullagh has been compared to two former lord mayors of Belfast: Otto Jaffé (1899-1900, 1904-1905) and William Pirrie (1896-1898), both in terms of their contribution to civic life in the city at the end of the nineteenth century and the sense of largesse they displayed when in public office. During their term of office, no expense was spared in the entertaining of visiting guests and dignitaries, and this largesse was paid for from their resources rather than the public purse.

McCullagh had good reason to be obliged to Otto Jaffé, a Jewish businessman. Jaffé had been lord mayor in 1899 and in 1904. In 1914, he proposed McCullagh for the office. The Jewish community in Belfast was small. In the nineteenth century, as pogroms in Russia and Poland increased, many Jews found their way to Belfast. The 1861 census recorded 52, which increased to 78 in 1881 and 273 in 1891. In 1850, Otto Jaffé's father had arrived from Hamburg in Germany and set up home in Belfast where he soon bought a very successful linen exporting business. By the 1890s, the Jewish community in Belfast had set up a Board of Guardians (1893), a Hebrew Ladies' Foreign Benevolent Society (1896), and a Hebrew National School in 1898.[116]

In 1877, Otto Jaffé, at 31 years old, took over the business from his father and the firm went from strength to strength. In a similar pattern to that of McCullagh and Pirrie, he

---

[116] J. Bradbury, *Celebrated Citizens of Belfast*, (Belfast, 2002), p. 46.

became involved in local government when he became a city councillor in 1894. He joined the Harbour Board and, along with the Pirries, he became a governor and benefactor of the Royal Victoria Hospital. He was knighted for his charitable work in the city in 1899 and contributed to the building of a new synagogue, which opened in Annesley Street near Carlisle Circus in 1901. His influence on McCullagh was significant. They were both enterprising businessmen in the city, and their paths often crossed. With the outbreak of war in 1914, Jaffé's German origins became a matter of concern for leading Belfast citizens; he left his adopted city and settled in London, where he died in 1929.

William Pirrie and Crawford McCullagh had more in common in terms of their development as city businessmen. Both had started at the bottom rung and had worked themselves to the top. Pirrie was one of the outstanding industrial leaders of his generation, while McCullagh was credited with being the largest ratepayer in the city. Both were self-made men and with a reputation of being 'men of action'.

Pirrie became a member of the Belfast Harbour Commissioners in 1893 and continued in that position until 1906. He had a natural interest in the port because of his shipping interests and acquired more land from the commissioners to develop the Harland and Wolff yard.[117] He joined the International Marine Syndicate formed in 1902, a trans-Atlantic syndicate with ambitions to control the Atlantic shipping business. Within this consortium, Pirrie's ever-increasing expansion plans became dependent on ever-increasing borrowings, and he risked being over-borrowed.

---

[117] H. Jefferson, *Viscount Pirrie of Belfast* (Belfast, 1948), p. 109.

In a financial bubble around shipping, Pirrie forestalled the concerns of others by keeping his cards close to his chest. By 1914, according to Moss and Hume, Pirrie 'had become a business dictator on a gigantic scale, and no one within the company could challenge his authority and skill. He would not countenance any failure. Consequently, his staff were terrified of him'. He kept all information and statistics to himself so that other members of the firm did not know how the business was faring.[118] Frequently, the annual reports of profits and losses were cooked – in a way that was legal – while the real financial state of the firm was concealed from shareholders and the board.[119]

## McCullagh and Pirrie on home rule

Both McCullagh and Pirrie grew their businesses under the shadow and threat of home rule. Pirrie initially thought that home rule for Ireland would be bad, not just for Ireland but also for Britain. The unionist fear of home rule was economic. Unionists believed that a Dublin parliament would endeavour to tax northern industries to subsidise southern enterprises, and so undermine the competitiveness of northern businesses. As a leading Belfast businessman, McCullagh shared this view.

By 1902, Pirrie saw some merit in the idea of home rule and could foresee Ireland exercising a measure of home rule within a Great British empire. He believed at the time that a

---

[118] M. Moss, J. Hume, *Shipbuilders to the World: 125 Years of Harland and Wolff*, Belfast, 1861-1986 (Belfast, 1986), 173.
[119] R. Johnstone, *Belfast: Portraits of a City*, (London, 1990), p. 122.

'continued government of Ireland from Westminster could be neither stable nor economical'.[120] Pirrie's British business colleagues, such as John and Owen Philipps of the Royal Mail Shipping Group, favoured a form of home rule. The Philipps had close ties with Harland and Wolff, and it was important for Pirrie to keep them onside.[121] As a staunch unionist, McCullagh's perspective never deviated.

After the 1910 general election, the Liberal Government espoused the home rule cause and Pirrie went along with it, perceiving that it was in the best interests of industrial Belfast and Ulster. In 1912, he hired the Ulster Hall for Winston Churchill, John Redmond and Joe Devlin to address a home rule gathering. The night before the meeting, unionist activists took over the Hall and refused to vacate the following day, forcing the home rule meeting to take place in a large marquee in the Celtic Football Grounds on 7 February 1912.[122]

Churchill had formerly given his backing to the unionist cause and now equivocated on the home rule idea. His position by 1912 was to support the notion of Irish self-government if it would facilitate a federalised United Kingdom. Speaking to an audience of about 7,000, Churchill admitted it was right for Ulster Unionists to insist upon their liberties but warned them against becoming 'the tool or catspaw of the Tory party in England'.[123] His words were not well received and, for their efforts, a few days later Pirrie and his wife were pelted with rotten eggs by a unionist mob when

---

[120] R.D.C. Black, *William James Pirrie,* in SMI, pp. 182-3.
[121] G. Simpson, in *History Ireland,* vol. 20, no. 2, 2012.
[122] Jefferson, p. 139.
[123] M. C. Rast, in *History Ireland,* vol 28, no 1, 2020.

they boarded a boat to return to Britain.

Later in the year, the Prime Minister, Asquith, introduced a Home Rule Bill, which resulted in a unionist revolt and the signing of the Belfast Covenant on 28 September 1912. The following month, on 23 October, Pirrie and six leading business figures publicly declared that 'the present Home Rule Bill is an honest endeavour to grabble with the problem, and should be passed into law.'[124]

Ulster was violently opposed to the Bill, which passed in parliament in 1914 but did not become law until after the 1914-18 war. It was later called the Home Rule Act and was subsequently replaced in 1920 with a new Act which gave Ireland two parliaments, one in Belfast, and the other in Dublin.

The war years were good for Harland and Wolff's shipping yards. Under Pirrie's directives, the peacetime enterprise was now on a war production footing. The yard produced warships and military hardware, and in March 1919 Pirrie became controller general of merchant shipbuilding.[125] By then, Harland and Wolff had completed 201,070 gross tons of merchant shipping, 120,000 tons more than anyone else. Under his stewardship, output rose nearly 50 percent by the end of the war. Politically, the events of the 1916 Easter Uprising in Dublin and its aftermath ended Pirrie's romance with home rule, and when the war ended in 1918, he was back in the unionist fold.

Pirrie was a late developer. Not interested in school or college, he had pestered his mother to allow him to take up a

---

[124] Jefferson, p. 141.
[125] G. Simpson, in *History Ireland*, issue 2, 2012, vol. 20.

'gentleman apprentice' at Harland and Wolff, and he rose swiftly through the ranks.[126] When Harland himself, and Gustave Wolff, retired from the active partnership, he was left in central control of the entire business.[127] His widowed mother gave him a compendium of maxims that he carried with him everywhere in later life.

One such maxim that he often quoted was, 'you have your own way to make. It depends on your exertions where you starve or not'.[128] McCullagh too began his career through an apprenticeship in the Bank Buildings in Belfast and he also often quoted advice that his mother had given him when he was setting out on life's journey.

Pirrie, like McCullagh, had a strong work ethic and, again like McCullagh, possessed a cheerful optimism and exercised good judgment in appointing able lieutenants. He had a feverish interest in innovation and sought new ways to stay ahead of the opposition. Like McCullagh, he viewed money not as an end but a means to an end.[129] Crawford McCullagh's contribution to Belfast was not unlike Pirrie's as both helped to make Belfast a major industrial and commercial centre and 'served to enhance the difference between Ulster and the rest of Ireland'.[130]

---

[126] Jefferson p. 311.
[127] J. McGuire, J. Quinn (eds.), *Dictionary of Irish Biography*, vol. 8, p. 147.
[128] Johnstone, p. 117.
[129] Jefferson, p. 302.
[130] E. Biagini, D. Mulhall (eds), *The Shaping of Modern Ireland* (Dublin, 2016), P. 183.

## The Irish Convention 1917

Halfway through the 1914-1918 war, the lord lieutenant appointed McCullagh to be the Director of Recruitment for the Northern Area. This prompted Lloyd George, when calling for an all-Ireland conference of both unionist and nationalist leaders, to invite McCullagh to attend the 1917 Convention, though he was no longer the lord mayor of Belfast, though leading businessman William Pirrie was deliberately omitted from the northern contingent. Yet with his strong commercial and business acumen, he might have made a valuable contribution to the all-Ireland Convention.

The attendees at the conference were a representative grouping of all shades of opinion in Ireland, and it was hoped that the delegates would arrive at a constitution for the future governing of Ireland within the United Kingdom.

Sinn Fein and the populous grouping now moving away from the Irish party (IIP) were refused membership of the Convention. The Ulster Unionist Council was initially reluctant to enter the Convention until Edward Carson convinced them that he had a guarantee from the prime minister, Lloyd George, that unless the Ulster Unionists were happy with Convention proposals, Britain would refuse to implement any Convention findings.[131]

The Convention gradually ground to a halt in the spring of 1918 after a limitless amount of time and energy resulted in no practical results. The one unanimous recommendation to emerge was the commitment to fully implement the Land Acts that would enable tenant farmers to acquire their

---

[131] F. Gallagher, *The Invisible island* (London, 1957), p. 129.

holdings.[132] Lord Londonderry, as one of the leading Unionists, gradually lost interest in the Convention's work. On the nationalist side, John Redmond became terminally ill and he died in March 1918. His successor as leader of the Irish Parliamentary Party, John Dillon, lacked the required energy and focus to progress matters. Outside Ireland, a massive crisis loomed in a shortage of manpower for the Allies in the war against Germany.

The Convention issued its final report in March, endorsed by 60 percent of the delegates. It had a key recommendation of a home rule solution for Ireland within a federal United Kingdom. Failing that, Ireland would have Dominion Status within the British Empire. The following month, the British Cabinet responded with their recommendation that involved a 'dual policy' of devolution and army conscription for Ireland.

The conscription element was a bridge too far for Irish nationalists and it was an excuse for others to revert to pre-ordained unionist positions which had been under stress during the previous nine months. In essence, the conscription idea afforded 'a watershed for Ulster unionists to withdraw securely into their northern citadel'.[133] With that withdrawal, McCullagh took the time to focus on his business concerns and the ongoing work of Belfast Corporation.

## Honours for Sir Crawford McCullagh

The war years (1914-18) were a critical time in the city's history. It was wartime, and there were daily consultations

---

[132] D. J. Owen, *History of Belfast* (London, 1921), p. 346.
[133] Cunningham, p.148.

between the military and the civil authorities. McCullagh was often called upon for decisive action on important matters. For services rendered, he was knighted in 1915 and he and his wife Margaret became honorary burgesses in 1917, with a citation dated 23 January that read 'as a mark of the appreciation of the citizens for the very able manner in which he discharged the responsible duties of lord mayor more especially after the declaration of war when he took the lead in every movement in which the Citizens could join to assist the Empire, her navy, and her army'.[134]

No less impressive was the citation for McCullagh's wife 'for the manner in which she discharged the responsible duties of lady mayoress in the years 1914, 1915, 1916', demonstrating 'ability and tact ... in the raising and application of very large sums of money for the alleviation of suffering, and the provision of comforts for the Sailors and Soldiers, of the Empire'.[135]

---

[134] *The Belfast book*, (Belfast, 1929), p. 12.
[135] Ibid.

# 4

# CIVIL WAR IN BELFAST

# 1920-1922

*Things fall apart; the centre cannot hold;*
*Mere anarchy is loosed upon the world ...*
W B Yeats (1920)

Crawford McCullagh's entry into parliament was preceded by
two years of unrelenting social and political unrest in the city
between 1920 and 1922. The economic depression after the
First World War had a crucial impact on the commercial life
of the city while the southern Government attempted to
choke city trade through guerrilla warfare and economic
boycott. There were 14,000 unemployed in 1919 and three
years later, this number had jumped to 30,000. The traditional
mainstay industries in the city failed and with a dangerous
political upheaval between 1920 and 1922 'Belfast seemed to
resemble more closely the capitals of states created out of the
wreck of the collapsed empires than the more stable cities of
north western Europe'.[136] It was then that Crawford
McCullagh entered parliament for the first time.

## City unrest

Belfast city between the summer of 1920 and late 1922 was a

---

[136] J. Bardon, *Belfast, an illustrated history* (Belfast, 1982), p.192.

virtual war zone when up to 500 inhabitants lost their lives and over 2,000 were seriously injured. This badly affected business in the city with the commercial centre suffering damages of £3 million. In that period, 10,000 were forced out of their place of work and 20,000 frightened out of their homes. There has been a modest reference to this in the past with academic interest in the period focusing on the Irish Republican Army (IRA) campaign, or the incarceration of Republicans on the prison ship *Argenta,* or, indeed, the exploits of the Ulster Special Constabulary (USC).[137]

Yet the eruption of violence in Belfast gave rise to 'bloodshed on an unprecedented scale'. The origins of the conflict can be traced back to the introduction of the Government of Ireland legislation in 1920 when the threat from the IRA 'flying columns' targeted Ulster-born police officers. The Protestant workers in the shipyards feared for their jobs while Unionist politicians stoked the fires of unrest by declaring that if the Government could not contend with the IRA, loyalists would take matters into their own hands.[138]

## The Belfast unemployed

Many Belfast Protestants who returned home after the war failed to be re-employed in the Belfast shipyard. Subsequently, 5,000 of them met at the Workman and Clark shipyard to seek the expulsion of 'non-loyal' (viz Catholics) workers and 'rotten Prods'. They also marched to Harland

---

[137] A. F. Parkinson, *Belfast's unholy war: the Troubles of the 1920s* and in A.F. Parkinson and E. Phoenix (eds), *Conflicts of the North of Ireland 1900-2000* (Dublin, 2010), p. 70.
[138] M. Farrell, *Northern Ireland: the Orange State* (London, 1976), p. 27.

and Wolff and, armed with crowbars and wooden staves, they chased Catholics and socialists from the yard. In the ensuing days, the Catholics retaliated by attacking the day trams that carried Protestant workers to the shipyards.

Industrial bullying spread from the shipyards to several other industrial and commercial premises in the city. Catholics were ejected from the Sirocco works, the linen mills, Musgrave's, Combe Barbour's and Mackies engineering works in west Belfast. Protestants, too, who were the minority workforce on the docks or in the catering industries, suffered intimidation and expulsion. Protestant trade union officials (comprising a quarter of all those evicted from the shipyards) found themselves intimidated and expelled from the workplace.[139] To fill their absence, temporary shop stewards were drawn from the ranks of loyalist vigilante committees who targeted socialist workers and trade unionists with death threats and arson attacks simply because they were 'rotten Prods'.[140]

The Westminster Government distanced itself from these events in Belfast. While the Government rightly condemned all forms of intimidation and industrial expulsion, it felt that it had no moral power to insist that employers should employ anyone based on them being 'Roman Catholic, Orangemen, or anyone else'.

Some of the worst atrocities happened in the heart of the city.[141] The busy shopping area of Castle Junction experienced

---

[139] A. Morgan, *Labour and Partition: the Belfast Working Class 1905-1923* (London, 1991), p. 269.
[140] A. F. Parkinson, *A Difficult Birth: the Early Years of Northern Ireland 1920-25* (Dublin, 2020), p.21.
[141] Ibid., p.57.

gunfire and witnessed stampeding crowds in Donegal Place, Royal Avenue and High Street. Some of this happened on the doorstep of Crawford McCullagh's business premises, wherein one mid-afternoon 'sudden shots were heard from the direction of Castle Street and a wild rush occurred. People sprinted in all directions, and crouched into doorways, and women ran frantically for shelter'.[142] In the last quarter of 1920, there was comparative peace in the city and only four people suffered violent deaths.[143]

By September 1920, a city curfew was in force. The *Irish News* reported that the tramcars ceased running before half-past nine and the military took up positions with barbed wire re-erected at York Street as civilians hurried homewards. By ten-thirty, the city streets were deserted and military patrols intercepted anyone out and about.

When the senior British civil servant, Sir Ernest Clark, arrived in Belfast on 15 September 1920, his function was to prepare the framework for the new Northern Ireland administration and address the city unrest by encouraging the re-employment of expelled Catholics and socialists in the shipyards. Rather than renew old employment, many Catholics had now taken up work on Belfast Corporation and worked on the city tramline reconstruction scheme, had emigrated to Scotland or sought work in the south of the country.

When the Government of Ireland Act became law on 23 December 1920, it transferred significant but not absolute powers from Westminster to new administrations in Dublin and Belfast. The loyalists reluctantly accepted the new

---

[142] *Irish News*, 1 September 1920.
[143] A. F. Parkinson, *A Difficult Birth: the Early Years of Northern Ireland 1920-25* (Dublin 2020), p.60.

legislation, although they had opposed any home rule measures in the past. The election campaign to the Belfast parliament was lengthy and intensely contested, and the outcome clear and decisive. All 40 Unionist candidates were elected, with Sinn Fein and other nationalists dividing up the remaining twelve seats.

## Formal opening of the Belfast parliament

The formal opening of the new parliament took place on 22 June 1921. The king arrived from Britain and allayed Unionist fears by underpinning the British connection and re-enforcing the link between Northern Ireland and Britain.[144]

The royal yacht sailed up Belfast Lough and the city centre came to a standstill to cheer on King George and Queen Mary. Tens of thousands lined the streets. Nationalists and Republicans boycotted the whole affair and missed the inspiring speech in the council chamber of the City Hall when the king made a heartfelt plea for peace and reconciliation. The visit lasted five hours with a colossal security presence. The immediate Republican response to the visit was to attack a military train as it returned south to Dublin. Four soldiers who had formed part of the cavalry escort for the king's visit were killed, along with two civilians and 80 of the 100 horses on the train.

---

144 *Belfast Telegraph*, 22 June 1921.

## The Belfast boycott

The response of the Dublin Republicans to the Government of Ireland Act 1920 was to direct their focus on the city of Belfast between the late summer of 1920 and the early summer of 1922, with the boycott of Belfast goods. The rationale behind it was the belief that imposing economic sanctions on the city would bring economic life there to a standstill. Not all Republicans agreed with it. The northern Republican, Ernest Blyth, considered that the 'blockade of Belfast' would destroy the very possibility of a united Ireland 'for ever'.[145]

The boycott was initially intended to put pressure on Ulster Loyalists to reinstate Catholics who had been driven from their workplaces by urging the boycott and destruction of goods produced in Belfast and the rest of the province. Southern members of the IRA monitored and directed boycott manoeuvres. Trains leaving the north were hijacked and a range of products, including such basics as bread and liqueur and linen goods, were confiscated or destroyed.

The local press reported a typical train hijack. 'While the train was slowly proceeding up the incline, a number of armed men appeared and jumped on the engine. They compelled the driver and the fireman to halt and stand by, and then approached the guard and procured from him his wage bill of invoices showing the forwarding station of the goods carried ... and the raiders went systematically through the fifty-odd wagons of the train, and removed oil, cart wheels, drapery and tea'.[146]

---

[145] C. Townsend, *The Partition* (New York, 2021), p. 168.
[146] *Irish News,* 10 May 1921.

During the first six months of 1922, violence erupted on the Belfast streets as 'evil men on both sides competed in their depravity'.[147] The north and south leaders, James Craig and Michael Collins, had sought a solution to the conflict through a peace agreement signed on 21 January 1922 whereby the boycott of northern goods was called off. In exchange, Catholics who were expelled from their work premises were to be reinstated. Such was the turmoil and heightened unrest in the city that the Craig-Collins pact came to nothing and the two leaders met again to agree to a second peace pact on 30 March 1922, which again proved futile.

Violence continued on the city streets. Loyalist gunmen targeted Catholics, and snipers and bombers were active in all areas. They spared nobody. When the shooting broke out in the city centre, people sought refuge in shops or jumped aboard passing trams.[148] The young, the infirm and the elderly were targeted along with people travelling to work. Many deaths were due to people being in the wrong place at the wrong time – people visiting shops, children playing games in the street. The IRA initially targeted police officers but overtly moved to sectarian attacks by bombing Protestant workers' tram-cars and burning commercial properties. Over 80 business premises were seriously damaged or destroyed in Belfast.

City workers took their life in their hands when crossing Belfast by tram. Citizens became victims of physical and verbal abuse, which often resulted in fatal shootings at the

---

[147] A. F. Parkinson, *Belfast's Unholy War: the Troubles of the 1920s;* in A.F. Parkinson and E. Phoenix (eds), *Conflicts in the North of Ireland 1900-2000* (Dublin, 2010), p.81.
[148] *Irish News* 25 April 1921.

hands of loyalist gunmen. With insufficient cover by the security forces, the city transport authorities fortified their trams with wire mesh on the outside to protect against stones, bottles and hand-grenades, and Mills bombs.[149]

## The Special Powers Act

The Special Powers Act came into force on 7 April 1922; it gave the Minister of Home Affairs the power to detain suspects and set up courts of immediate execution. The Act had nine sections and thirty regulations, making it complicated to implement. Several of the powers for preserving peace, law and order were transferred from the judiciary to the government authorities. The Act was comprehensive in scope and allowed for a special court to immediately convene for hasty execution.

There were exacting penalties for definite offenses – the death penalty for throwing bombs and individual flogging for carrying arms without sanction. The Minister of Home Affairs had discretionary powers to take any steps he perceived necessary to maintain law and order. He also had the authority to delegate any of his powers to his under-secretary or any officer of the newly established Royal Ulster Constabulary. In effect, 'under the Act, the Minister of Home Affairs could vest all his powers in a single RUC constable, who could then lock up everybody else in the country including the Minister, and would be in perfect accordance

---

[149] Mills bombs were the first modern fragmentation grenades used by the British Army in the 1st and 2nd World Wars.

with the law.'[150]

Unionists originally found fault with the legislation because they perceived it to be too lengthy and because it required one section in the Act viz 'The home secretary shall have power to do what he likes or else let somebody else do what he likes for him'.[151]

That being so, politicians like Robert Lynn, MP for West Belfast, argued that the Government had not gone far enough and wondered was 'civilisation going to be allowed to exist, or is there going to be anarchy'.[152] Relative peace returned to Belfast in the summer of 1922, but not before May and June when the IRA gave orders for the assassination of the Unionist MP, William Twaddell, and General Sir Henry Wilson. Both were shot dead in street attacks.

The violence settled down in the autumn of 1922. Republican suspects were interred because of the Emergency Powers legislation and when the civil war broke out in the south in August, the IRA volunteers moved south meaning loyalists had fewer people to confront in the city precincts.

## The end of the boycott

The boycott, though rigorous and persistent, did not result in economic disaster. While small firms experienced substantial financial loss, the larger commercial and manufacturing enterprises in the city traded with Great Britain and beyond rather than with the rest of Ireland, which lessened the

---

[150] O. Dudley Edwards, *The Sins of our Fathers: Roots of Conflict in Northern Ireland* (Dublin, 1970), p. 105.
[151] T. Wilson (ed), *Ulster Under Home Rule* (London, 1955), pp. 47-48.
[152] J. Bardon, *Belfast, an Illustrated History* (Belfast, 1982), p.201.

impact of the boycott on them. Ulster traders and businessmen formed an Ulster Trades Defence Association in May 1921 and organised a counter-boycott campaign to undermine the southern economy. While the economic damage was not inconsiderable, the major thrust of the boycotts was to further alienate northern Unionists from southern Nationalists and it further harassed the beleaguered Belfast's minority Catholic community.[153]

It also 'contributed to the destruction of one aspect of Irish unity – the commercial unity of the country based on the importance of Belfast as a distribution centre for the majority of Ireland. In 1924, exports from the six to the 26 counties were half the level of 1920'.[154] While much of Belfast industry depended on raw materials and export markets, its links with the rest of Ireland in the matter of retail, wholesale and distribution were exceedingly important.[155] The boycott of industries in the city was violent in its execution, but ultimately it failed in its aim to disrupt the northern economy over the long term.

Several members of the new Belfast Government had business interests in the city and had easy access to government ministers, including the prime minister, James Craig. A fortunate consequence of this was that the new Government felt empowered to initiate a Loans Guarantee Act in 1922, whereby loans made by the banks to business

---

[153] A. F. Parkinson, *Belfast's Unholy War: the Troubles of the 1920s;* in A.F. Parkinson and E. Phoenix (eds), *Conflicts in the North of Ireland 1900-2000* (Dublin, 2010), p. 77.
[154] D. Kennedy, *The Widening Gulf: Northern Attitudes to the Independent Irish State 1919-49* (Belfast, 1988), pp 88-89.
[155] P. Ollerenshaw, *Business and Industry* in Alvin Jackson (ed), *The Oxford Handbook of Modern Irish History,* p.157.

concerns would be guaranteed by the Government. Many business owners in the city availed of the initiative. It is not known if Sir Crawford McCullagh, as a prominent businessman, availed of this scheme.[156]

# 5

# CRAWFORD McCULLAGH IN PARLIAMENT

## 1921-1925

*Politics is still the greatest and most honourable adventure.*
Lord Tweedsmuir

### The Belfast Parliament – background

The triumph of Sinn Fein in the General Election of 1918 and the ensuing Anglo-Irish war led to the Government of Ireland Act (1920) which partitioned Ireland into two parliamentary areas. The Northern Ireland area comprised six counties: Antrim, Armagh, Down, Fermanagh, Londonderry and Tyrone, along with the parliamentary boroughs of Belfast and Londonderry, with a representative parliament in Belfast city. A parliament in Dublin represented the 26 counties of Independent Ireland.

The Government of Ireland Act allowed for a Council of Ireland to meet with the intention, in time, of promoting an all-Ireland parliament. The Council comprised 20 members drawn from the parliaments of Northern and Independent Ireland and the intention was for delegates to discuss matters of mutual concern, including the administration of services. Sir Crawford McCullagh was delegated as one of the northern representatives to sit on the Council, but in fact, the Council was never convened.

The Northern parliament comprised a House of Commons and an upper House, the Senate, and the representative make-up comprised 52 members who then elected 24 members to the Senate. Ministers could speak in both houses and vote in the house where they were a member. The Northern Ireland parliament was largely a part-time affair for representatives and it met for a couple of months every year. Its dominant function was to endorse government policy.[157]

The overriding role of the Commons regarding legislation was a passive one, as the elected politicians were impotent to raise questions around a litany of 'exempted' or 'reserved services'. The list of these 'reserved services' was long. It included matters of the Crown, peace and war, matters to do with the armed forces, foreign treaties, any trade matters outside Northern Ireland, currency matters, concerns arising out of the Supreme Court of Northern Ireland, the registration of deeds, the postal service, stamp designs and savings banks.

All these powers were the preserve of the imperial parliament in London, but it was intended that these 'exempt' and 'reserved' powers and services would be transferred to a newly elected all-Ireland assembly, when Irish unity would eventually be achieved. In the meantime, under Section 23 of the 1920 Act, Northern Ireland was expected to contribute to the imperial coffers while the Government in London took from the province's reserved taxation the cost of the reserved services in Northern Ireland.

---

[157] See N. Mansergh, *The Government of Northern Ireland* (London, 1936), pp. 125-168.

## Political neophytes

The politicians who made up the new Northern Parliament were political neophytes with little initiative or know-how in the administration of a new state. With a few exceptions, they were 'not politically mature enough to assume the running of a new Northern Ireland state and they had no coherent philosophy on how to govern a state they had neither expected nor wanted'.[158] Most MPs had little to contribute in political debate and parliament became a talking shop where 'parish pump' politics and the raising of local constituency issues was their primary concern. In this, they displayed an 'essential amateurishness' and regularly were 'embarrassingly ill-informed'.[159] While deep religious divisions underlay Unionist and Nationalist parliamentary representation, the real divide was between 'MPs representing Belfast and those sitting for the rest of the six counties'.[160]

The newly established Government quickly came to understand that the Belfast Corporation was a law onto itself in many respects. Prime Minister James Craig cautioned the Junior Minister of Home Affairs in a dispute that arose with the Corporation on housing policy and advised the minister that 'we always have to bear in mind that the city represents in many respects one half of Northern Ireland and therefore requires careful handling'.[161]

There were few farming representatives in parliament; they were more concerned about holding on to their homesteads

---

[158] History, vol.60, no 199 (1975), p. 215.
[159] Ibid., p. 33.
[160] Ibid.
[161] Ibid., p. 40.

rather than airing grievances in Belfast. Class division and distinction bothered some Unionist MPs when working-class people of meagre ability were elected to parliament and were 'unable to transcend their Unionist and Protestant origins'. Northern Ireland returned thirteen MPs to the Westminster parliament, eleven of whom were Unionists. Here, the Unionists organised their parliamentarians with a chairman, secretary, and whip, taking their cue from the Conservative party. Yet, their influence in the imperial parliament was limited because the freedom to comment on the affairs of Northern Ireland was forbidden lest any comment on any potential controversial matters would rebound on Anglo-Irish relations.

## McCullagh in parliament

Sir Crawford McCullagh was elected to represent South Belfast for five years (1921-25) in the new parliament, which met for the first time in City Hall. In parliament, he contributed to every session but failed to be re-elected in 1925. His contributions mainly reflected the concerns of Belfast Corporation and ranged across housing (1921), grants (1921), finance (1921), the Special Powers Bill (1923), estimates, the parliamentary budget (1922, 1923, 1924), the Imperial Contribution (1922), the Proportional Representation bill (1922), income tax, reform of local elections (1922), the Belfast Corporation Bill (1923), trains, buses, gas works, milk and meat hygiene, coal, markets, pensions, the Education Bill (1923), valuations (1923), the Housing Bill (1923), the importance of private enterprise (1924), the work rate of labourers (1924), the inadequacy of the Housing Bill (1924), subsidies (1922), his ambitions (May 1924), entertainment tax (1924). It was quite a list, but arguably reflected nothing other than a run-of-the-mill contribution to local politics.

When McCullagh arrived in parliament on 23 June 1921, he was one of 13 politicians elected from the Northern Ireland parliament to the Council of Ireland, a statutory body established under the Government of Ireland Act in 1920, intended to be an all-Ireland, law-making authority with limited jurisdiction over Northern Ireland and Southern Ireland. As a former lord mayor of Belfast and a noted businessman, it was unsurprising that McCullagh would be elected, but the Council never met and it was abolished in 1925.

From the start, McCullagh showed energy and enthusiasm in contributing to parliamentary work. Besides being elected to the Council of Ireland, fellow members voted for him to be a member of the House of Commons Kitchen and Refreshment Rooms Committee.

The first home of the new Northern Ireland parliament was City Hall (Fig.5) where the first meeting of the parliament was held in June 1921.

5. City Hall.

Shortly afterward, the parliament moved to the Assembly College on Botanic Avenue, the home of the Theological College of the Presbyterian Church. A site for a new parliamentary building was located at Stormont, but there were objections to the building within the Unionist ranks and particularly from Crawford McCullagh who argued that the proposed building would be too costly to build and it was too far from the city centre. The Prime Minister, Sir James Craig, went ahead with the proposed building project, which eventually accommodated not just the parliament but the civil service and the law courts. In December 1921, the Stormont estate and Stormont Castle were purchased and the foundation stone for the new parliamentary buildings was laid on 19 May 1928.

Early in parliamentary debates, McCullagh manifested a strong concern for housing developments in Belfast city. In referring to such matters in parliament, he demonstrated a pragmatic turn of mind on the housing question when there was a tacit reluctance by the Home Office to satisfactorily engage with the problem.

McCullagh urged the cabinet to 'hustle quicker', arguing that the Government must face up to the 'real facts' and get 'down to business'. He felt there was too much talk and little constructive work done to ease the growing problem of inadequate housing across the province. McCullagh saw a need to challenge the British Government on transferred services. He chided fellow politicians who hid behind a plea that they could do nothing until the southern parliament was set up. McCullagh felt many services could be transferred at once and it was useless to meet and just talk. He asserted that 'if we have the power, we ought to exercise it as soon as possible'.[162]

By the end of September 1921, McCullagh, with his business background, found himself on the Public Accounts Committee in the Commons, where he voiced his concern that all designated tax revenue should apply to the area for which it was collected. He had a particular interest in the tax that was collected for the maintenance of roads and insisted that when that tax was collected, it should not disappear into the general tax pool and be dispersed elsewhere. McCullagh had a huge personal interest in the developing car market in the city and was aware that Belfast city had collected £45k to lodge with the Roads Advisory Committee for Northern Ireland. Sir Dawson Bates assured him that the £45k would be ring-fenced and used for road maintenance.[163]

---

[162] Stormontpapers.ahds.ac.uk (accessed 25 March 2020), 1, pp. 111-12.
[163] Stormontpapers.ahds.ac.uk (accessed 25 March 2020), 1, pp. 205-6.

## Belfast housing

Eager to be engaged in parliamentary affairs, McCullagh became chairman of the joint Senate and the House of Commons Ways and Means Committee. This committee handled Notices of Motion, Local Bills, and Standing Orders. In December 1921, he was on his feet in the House of Commons, questioning the Home Affairs minister on the provisions that had been made for the subsidy due to be paid under the 1919 Housing Act. Belfast Corporation was already engaged in building social housing, but he insisted that if subsidy monies were not forthcoming, the Belfast housing scheme would have to stop and that 'great numbers will be thrown out of work'.

The Home Affairs minister, Dawson Bates, defended the current situation and accused the Corporation of not formally approaching the cabinet for money; it would seem now that the Corporation had not sufficiently protected itself to secure the money before it embarked on its building scheme.[164] While the Local Government Board (hereafter LGB) had insisted that the houses should be built, there was no reference in the Government estimates for money to be set aside for the scheme. Belfast Corporation, it seemed, had embarked on a building scheme without securing the money. McCullagh rejected the accusation, reiterating that the parliament had committed to underwrite the money.

The Second Session of the NI parliament opened in March 1922 and with a city experiencing the turmoil of social unrest, McCullagh continued to seek finance for house building. He asserted that the financial arrangements of the

---

[164] Stormontpapers.ahds.ac.uk (accessed 25 March 2020), 1, pp. 481-2.

1920 Act were inadequate and that house building ought to be carried out through private enterprise. However, private enterprise was slow to become involved because of government restrictions. The standard of housing demanded by the LGB was way beyond the means of Belfast working men, with the average cost of a house being £1,000. The Government refused to modify the standards and consequently the rents demanded were prohibitive.

McCullagh pointed out that the Corporation could help individuals through the Small Dwellings Acquisition Act whereby the corporation could advance 90% of the entire cost of the houses. He noted that a huge source of finance could be tapped in an initiative in the Ulster Savings Certificate, now promoted by the current Minister of Finance, Hugh Pollock.

While money was not forthcoming for housing schemes in Belfast, McCullagh was critical of the proposed £50k in the Government estimates for the erection of a new parliament building at Stormont (Fig.6). In March 1922, McCullagh expressed concerns about the amount of money estimated and was sceptical about the amount of money needed to modernise Stormont Buildings. Not only was the money extravagant, but he considered the site unsuitable for the housing of necessary ancillary services like the law courts and administrative offices. He believed the Government needed to locate a new site altogether.[165]

In May 1922, McCullagh reflected on the financial scale of running the new Government. He knew that public opinion was concerned that they had set the parliament up on too

---

[165] Stormontpapers.ahds.ac.uk (accessed 27 March 2020), 2, p. 272.

grand a scale, but dismissed any idea that they paid government ministers too much. In his opinion, ministerial pay was adequate and was but a fraction of what it took to run a modern state. He also doubted if the administrative staff could be reduced.

## The Imperial Fund

McCullagh considered that the solution to the high cost of running the Government could be found by reducing Northern Ireland's contribution to the Imperial Fund. The contribution expected from Northern Ireland was too high and 'absolutely wrong'. In Northern Ireland, state revenues in the province had substantially fallen, and he considered that the contribution to the Imperial Fund should not exceed three million pounds rather than the eight million demanded.

The Westminster Government had already acknowledged this and had given a rebate of two million pounds. McCullagh referred to the Joint Exchequer Board set up to determine the amount that Northern Ireland should contribute and believed that the province should only contribute what was workable without parliament shirking the province's financial responsibilities. He believed that the entire tax system was 'topsy-turvy'. McCullagh argued that there was sufficient surveillance in parliament to judiciously observe how the Government was meeting its spending obligations and that with the reform of the tax system the Government could give 'some relief to those people who are now paying such huge sums in income tax'.[166]

---

[166] Stormontpapers.ahds.ac.uk (accessed 29 March 2020), 2, pp. 661-64.

## Proportional representation (PR)

The theory behind the proportional representation system of elections was that it allowed elected bodies and individuals to accurately mirror the electorate itself and elect candidates proportionally. It originated in nineteenth-century Europe, whereby seats were allocated to political parties using a simple mathematical formula in proportion to their share of the vote. In Britain, Thomas Hare, a political scientist, devised an alternative system to secure the proportional representation of all classes in society, including minorities in the House of Commons and other electoral assemblies.

His system was extended to Ireland for the local elections in 1919-20 and the general election in 1921. It was based on the single transferable vote in multi-member constituencies, a process whereby voters could nominate their preferred choice of candidate. Candidates could win their seats by obtaining an electoral quota arrived at by counting the votes and transferring lower preferences. A plethora of complex rules that nobody quite understood surrounded the counting of votes to decide the outcome. The new Northern Ireland state found the system unsatisfactory in contrast to what happened in Independent Ireland, where the PR system was incorporated into the constitutions of 1922 and 1937.

In parliament, McCullagh spoke out against PR. He welcomed the Local Government Bill, which set out to scrap the system entirely and he put on record his strong feeling regarding the matter. He dismissed the system based on what he had observed during two elections. McCullagh argued that if the system was not repealed, there 'will be the greatest difficulty in getting sufficient candidates to contest any elections in future'.[167] He was not alone in thinking this and in June 1922, the Proportional Representation Bill put an end to PR and McCullagh was entirely in favour of its removal.[168]

Northern politicians viewed the system with suspicion, and Unionist politicians suspected it was a Trojan horse that would undermine their capacity to govern. They had a good reason for thinking this. R J Lawrence, writing later in the century, pointed out that the Government at the time faced a 'fanatical opposition' when 'gunmen and gangsters tried to wreck the regime by murder and arson' and 'southern Ireland sought to strangle it by a trade embargo' and 'Roman Catholic prelates refused to recognise it'.

## Financing the Government

The financial provisions of the 1920 Act under which Northern Ireland was to pay nearly £8 million to the imperial coffers looked to most observers like 'financial strangulation' of the country. Independent Ireland subsequently escaped the imposition by negotiating the 1921 Treaty, leaving the Unionist politicians and McCullagh to complain that the financial arrangements for the Northern Ireland administration were 'unrealistic and inequitable' and that they failed to meet the increasing and necessary financial needs of the province.

The Imperial Government in London harboured a different view of the matter, suspecting Northern Ireland politicians and officials of 'attempting to spurge off the British tax payer while

---

[167] Stormontpapers.ahds.ac.uk (accessed 29 March 2020), 2, pp. 838-40.
[168] Stormontpapers.ahds.ac.uk (accessed 10 April 2020), 2, pp. 837-8.

enjoying regional autonomy'. The result was that the Northern Ireland parliament continued the everyday business of administrating the province as best they could. In the long run and during the inter-war period, the gross imperial contribution diminished to 'nearly nothing' when the account was 'taken of British subsidies to the Northern Ireland unemployment fund and other substantial transfers. In effect, the true imperial contribution was negative in most years and negative for the period as a whole'.[169]

The parliament in London was happy enough with the arrangement, as it allowed them to continue to keep an aloof distance between themselves and the Belfast administration. The price for this meant that there was sluggish economic development in the province with a hands-off approach by London in Northern Ireland affairs.

The aloof distancing of London from Belfast suited the Unionist leadership. It meant that there was no objection from Westminster when the Belfast Government removed the proportional representation system in both the local elections in 1922 and the parliamentary elections in 1929. The Home Office in London had reservations about the Education Amendments Bills of 1925 and 1930, but did not intervene. In the long run, however, any perceived advantages of a devolution model of local self-government for Northern Ireland were set at naught as the province adopted, as of right, British social services while economic initiatives created financial integration 'as complete as if the union had never been modified by the passing of the act of 1920'.[170]

---

[169] J. Johnston, *Irish Historical Studies,* No. 31 (1953), p. 288.
[170] Ibid.

## Belfast Corporation Bill 1923

When the Belfast Corporation Bill came before parliament for a second reading, it offered McCullagh an opportunity to give an extensive and exhaustive summary of the provisions. The Bill was a comprehensive overview of the Corporation's functions and the need for extensive new powers. There were many petitions lodged against the proposed measures and McCullagh addressed the ratepayers' concerns about municipal trading and the fears of those apprehensive about new corporation powers.

McCullagh argued that the local acts needed to be brought up-to-date and that this would affect several services – trams, buses, gasworks, chemical works, chemist shops, the provision of milk and meat, coal, and the sale of markets. The city sought to put more buses on the road in and around the city as it didn't have the money to lay down expensive tram lines.[171]

The gasworks in the city were a huge commercial success. While coal was imported, gas was cheaper in Belfast than in any other place in the UK. The huge gasworks produced more gas than was necessary to meet the needs of the city, so the Bill's provisions would allow the city to sell gas to neighbouring districts. In his remarks, McCullagh conceded that the Corporation was seeking very extensive powers, and seeking such powers was justified to bring local acts up-to-date.

The business of running the tramways was of particular concern to the Corporation which owned the tramways and wished to build lines out from the city, parallel to the railways. Naturally, the railway authorities were anxious that the proposed new tram lines wouldn't interfere with rail

---

[171] Stormontpapers.ahds.ac.uk (accessed 17 April 2020), 3, pp. 219-220.

revenue. The city wanted to extend the tramway as far as the Dundonald Cemetery and McCullagh, with wry humour, reasoned that there was 'great traffic on that route every day'. Other routes also needed to be developed and McCullagh argued it was essential to develop a line from the city out to Stormont buildings to facilitate the workmen and, in due course, the 'vast army of officials that would be located in Parliament House'.

The health of the city's population was of particular concern. He drew attention to the fact that the Corporation had plans to purchase the north of Ireland chemical works to manufacture residuals. Arrangements had been made with city chemists for the dispensing of health medicines to the public during the day or night and the Corporation sought to extend the number of chemist shops in the city.

There were concerns in the city regarding the delivery of milk and meat into Belfast. The Corporation sought the power to inspect such products before they were distributed throughout the city area. Twenty percent of the meat coming into the Belfast abattoir was affected by dreaded tuberculosis, a contagious infection caused by bacteria in the lungs. McCullagh advised the parliament that there was a tremendous concern about the delivery of unhygienic milk, which was opened at railway stations and in the streets, and transferred to milk cans. The Corporation wanted to take incoming milk to depots in the city where it could be properly handled to avoid contamination, removing the several milk markets located in the city area.

## City rates and housing

Belfast city councillors were always concerned about city rates and, on 3 May 1923, McCullagh raised their concerns in parliament. He pointed out that when merchants and manufacturers improved their properties in the city, it provoked enormous increases in their poor law valuations which were out of proportion to others who had properties in the same area. Consequently, many overdue improvements were put on hold. McCullagh wanted the Government to address the matter because property valuation in the city needed to be overhauled.

New, private dwelling houses were valued at a much higher rate than similar houses built before the war. McCullagh considered that this was unfair, as the high cost of building construction penalised homeowners enough. The present situation retarded the erection of private dwellings in the city and this impinged on the development of the city itself.

In response to McCullagh's observations, the Minister of Finance, Hugh Pollock, defended the status quo regarding the city rates, arguing that any extra measures to deal with the matter would be premature in the absence of expert knowledge and general evidence from the community.[172]

In the same parliamentary session, McCullagh expressed his satisfaction that the Government was committed to working on a new Housing Bill, and happily they were not merely considering an extension of the English Housing Act. He acknowledged that appreciable work was already underway to build houses for the workers of Belfast. However, he pointed out that bricklayers were in short supply

---

[172] Stormontpapers.ahds.ac.uk (accessed 17 April 2020), 3, pp. 704-8.

and that money needed to be spent on housing development in the current financial year. He believed that private enterprise could become involved in building houses if there was sufficient subsidy to buoy up the market. He alleged that many builders in Belfast owned land, but they would not build houses because the price of labour and materials was too high and it was impossible to make a reasonable return.[173]

## Corporation pensions

McCullagh took a leading role in the third reading of the Corporation Bill on 12 June 1923 and, drawing on his own long experience as a member of the Corporation, he believed that Corporation workers should be entitled to a pension. He acknowledged that the current situation was very unsatisfactory, whereby an employee, hoping for a pension, was at the mercy of the Corporation when he retired. With the current practice, an official on retirement had no security. McCullagh called for legislation that would enable all public officials who were engaged weekly or were salaried to have a pension. However, he conceded that there was a need for a full actuarial report to assess what it would cost. If an employee had friends in the Corporation, they could do well, otherwise any pension was at the whim and mercy of its members.

McCullagh wanted a legislated contributory pension scheme for all public officials. Workers in the Corporation should not have to beg or canvas for their pensions and he sought developments like those in Britain under the Local Government and Other Officers Superannuation Act of

---

[173] Stormontpapers.ahds.ac.uk (accessed 17 April 2020), 3, pp. 1065-7.

1922. In speaking thus, McCullagh was at pains to point out that he spoke on his own behalf and he had no mandate from the Corporation. He thought the English system was a good one as it required officials to contribute to their pension.[174]

McCullagh's concern for the rank-and-file Corporation official did not extend to civil servants. On 6 November 1923, the matter of houses for civil servants who transferred from Dublin and elsewhere into Belfast became a matter of contention. The Corporation had a policy of not providing a house for any official unless he had lived in Belfast since 1914, because they built houses for Belfast men and them alone. Yet, civil servants who were parachuted in from outside to help establish and run the new state lacked the means to buy a house or even rent on affordable terms. McCullagh was opposed to granting civil servants any concessions not offered to other people. He believed civil servants were well enough paid and was opposed to propping up a privileged class.[175]

## The Government Housing Bill

The Housing Bill was a matter of tremendous concern for McCullagh. The Government believed that introducing the Bill would result in the delivery of much-needed housing in the city. McCullagh warned it would fail to do so. He again insisted that there was a problem building houses in Belfast that could only be addressed when private developers were encouraged to enter the housing market as they had done in

---

[174] Stormontpapers.ahds.ac.uk (accessed 20 April 2020), 3, pp. 1429-1432.
[175] Stormontpapers.ahds.ac.uk (accessed 20 April 2020), 3, pp. 1712-16.

the years before the First World War. McCullagh observed that the housing problem was not peculiar to Belfast, but was prevalent in every large industrial centre across the north of Ireland.

The fundamental problem was the extraordinarily high price of building houses. In the past, Belfast had the lowest building costs in the British Isles. Now, they were higher than in many other parts of the United Kingdom. McCullagh elaborated on this by referring to a trip that he had previously taken with other members of the Corporation when they visited large industrial centres in Britain, the purpose being to inquire about housing conditions in Britain.

The visit revealed that at the lower end of the market, housing rents were twice as high in Britain than in Belfast, and at the upper end of the housing market, Belfast rents were one and a half times lower. The reasons for this were found in the large tracts of ground that were available to build upon in the Belfast region. Building materials were cheaper in Belfast than anywhere else and were sourced within the city boundary, with no handling costs. Cement was cheap. Timber prices were lower than across the Channel. Building by-laws were less stringent. Municipal rates were lower and, above all, there was an abundance of labour. All this combined to make Belfast city the cheapest place to build houses in the United Kingdom.

In January 1923, the Corporation sent another delegation to British cities only to discover that houses in Belfast were now twenty-five percent more expensive than those in Nottingham and Leicester. The cost of building materials in Belfast had risen, but the input from labour was less than elsewhere. The Corporation had endeavoured to keep the price of houses down through open competition, an building houses by direct labour. McCullagh further considered that a proposal that local authorities could give a rebate in rates up to five years was a dangerous principle in the Bill.[176]

McCullagh gave a personal undertaking that he would monitor house prices to avoid any profiteering by builders under the Small Dwellings Acquisition Act. It was agreed that the Corporation would give a grant of £40 per person to build a house in Belfast and the Government would augment that with a grant of £60, giving a total subsidy of £100, to be given to the builder. The grant would be repaid in small instalments every year, initially by the builder and, as and when he sold the house, the purchaser got the benefit of the original grant and became responsible for the annuities.[177]

During the parliamentary session in March 1924, Sir Robert Lynn accused the Government and the Belfast Corporation of demoralizing the building trade in Belfast city. Lynn maintained Corporation houses cost two-thirds more than any that were built by a private builder. The insinuation was that the Corporation couldn't be trusted to build houses; McCullagh continued to assert that even with the current subsidy, private builders couldn't build them to be sold at an economic price, or rent them for an economic return. Even with the subsidy, the price of a house in Northern Ireland was more expensive than a similar house in Great Britain.

McCullagh, always the pragmatist, wanted to know what could be done to remedy the situation. The supply of housing was too low. The Government had hoped that by implementing the Housing Bill, the supply of houses would

---

[176] Stormontpapers.ahds.ac.uk (accessed 20 April 2020), 3, pp. 1755-59.
[177] Stormontpapers.ahds.ac.uk (accessed 20 April 2020), 3, pp. 1996-2000.

dramatically increase. However, the number of plans lodged with the Corporation complying with regulations and qualifying for the subsidy was a mere 188, way below the normal number.

McCullagh was clear that the Housing Bill hadn't worked, and the Corporation and the Government couldn't stand idly by when people were clamouring for houses. He had no faith in government officials and civil servants to remedy matters. What was needed were cheaper houses that the people could afford. The Corporation was doing its bit – they were now building concrete houses.

## Building enterprise by the Corporation

McCullagh believed that the concrete house offered the possibility of using semi-skilled labour. However, when this was attempted, the bricklayers refused to lay the bricks to build the chimneys, and the carpenters refused to insert doors and other woodwork. Skilled men walked off the job, so the initiative of concrete housing had to stop.

Another initiative was then attempted – building houses with concrete blocks to keep prices down. A block represented six bricks. The Corporation got the machinery and put down the plant, with the Government paying eight percent of the wages. But this didn't work either because the bricklayers insisted on laying the same daily amount of bricks (now blocks) as previously. Across in Britain, bricklayers laid 2,000 bricks a day, while McCullagh informed Government that in Ireland 800 - 1000 bricks were the norm. The Corporation had tried and failed, despite the provision of housing in the city being its number one priority.[178]

The concern for housing Belfast people was still high on McCullagh's agenda when, on 10 April 1924, he estimated Belfast needed at least 5,000 new homes. The Corporation consistently maintained that the £40 subsidy should go to the owner or renter of the house, though McCullagh believed that the overall subsidy of £100 would not galvanize the market. Public bodies needed to stop building houses, and he called for an end to the letter-writing of bureaucrats that did nothing to facilitate house building. The cost of building was too high: the price of timber was rising and wages were due to go up on 1 July 1924.

Despite this, he argued that the Bill should be given a fair try, though nobody appeared to have the answer to the housing crisis; thousands were without homes of any kind. When Sir Dawson Bates introduced the Housing Bill in November 1923, Belfast alone had a shortfall of 8,000 - 10,000 dwellings, and houses for ordinary workers fetched prohibitive rents. McCullough believed they could solve the problem through private enterprise and if that failed, the Corporation and the Government had no choice but to come to the rescue.[179]

On 21 May 1924, the budget estimates came to parliament for discussion.[180] McCullough, amid groans of boredom from fellow members, raised the housing problem again and argued, 'I would not be myself if I did not speak on housing on every opportunity'.[181] He defended the Corporation's

---

[178] Stormontpapers.ahds.ac.uk (accessed 20 April 2020) 4, pp. 39-64.

[179] Stormontpapers.ahds.ac.uk (accessed 20 April 2020), 4, p. 679.

[180] Stormontpapers.ahds.ac.uk (accessed 21 April 2020), 4, pp. 1073-77.

[181] Stormontpapers.ahds.ac.uk (accessed 21 April 2020), 4, p. 1074.

house-building schemes. He said they had built houses when the private sector had failed to do so. They had built and almost completed sufficient houses to almost accommodate double the population of Carrickfergus. They had never wanted to build houses, but only did so out of necessity. He illustrated how the smallest house that could qualify for a government subsidy had no bath, and no hot or cold water. The cheapest would cost around £350 and the current subsidy grant that could be claimed was insufficient.

McCullagh insisted the Corporation was sick and tired of building houses; they had built a better type of house and had endeavoured to reduce the price. He believed it was possible to build a house for which the working man could pay a rent of between 6s and 8s but he admitted he didn't know how this could be achieved. He called for roundtable talks with the Government, the Corporation, and the labour unions to work it out.

On 4 November 1924, an amendment to the Housing Act was introduced which relieved all outstanding difficulties between the Corporation and the Government. The Corporation had objected to paying builders who had built houses and sold them with profit. The amendment gave the Corporation license to refuse the grant to those who sold houses at the full price, either before or after the Housing Act became law. McCullagh expressed his gratitude to the Government on the matter and pledged that any difficulties had now been resolved and that house building in the city would progress at a rapid rate.[182]

---

[182] Stormontpapers.ahds.ac.uk (accessed 21 April 2020), 4, pp. 1550-1573.

## Tax matters

Besides the housing crisis in Belfast, another bug-bear for McCullagh was the higher rate of tax on entertainment. He considered entertainment tax was a regressive tax on the less well-off. He had vested business interests in entertainment outlets in the city and considered that Northern Ireland had a higher taxation regime on entertainments compared to Britain. The reference to entertainment tax was not lost on the Minister of Finance, Hugh Pollock, who was aware of McCullagh's involvement in picture houses. Pollock assured McCullagh that the entertainment tax that affected picture houses also affected other social recreation activities, such as football matches. He made it clear that he was 'not for turning' on any such pleading, and he intended to keep as much money as possible in the Government coffers.

On 26 May 1924, there was further mention of the entertainment tax. McCullagh raised a point of order re the tax, which had not been reduced to the same level as in Britain, and he informed the minister that this was the source of widespread dissatisfaction. He demanded to know when the matter could be raised properly in the commons. He referred to the Colwyn Commission:[183] the principle embedded there meant that if there was a tax increase in Britain, Northern Ireland ought also to expect a similar rise. Conversely, if taxes were to reduce in Britain, a similar reduction should follow in Northern Ireland.[184]

---

[183]The Colwyn Committee was a special arbitration set up to report on what contribution the Northern Ireland parliament should make to the Imperial Fund.

[184] Stormontpapers.ahds.ac.uk (accessed 21 April 2021), 4, p. 1118.

## Assessment

In a ground-breaking work in 1965, R J Lawrence wrote of the 'profound apathy' that was experienced in the Northern Ireland parliament, making it 'wholly ineffective' in the early years of the century as neither the majority Unionists nor the minority Nationalists had sought a home rule parliament for a mere six counties.[185]

McCullagh's contribution to the first parliament was indeed unremarkable. He, along with other MPs, disputed the amount of money to be paid to the Imperial Fund and rejected any notion from the public that ministers were paid too much. As a staunch Unionist, he identified proportional representation as a threat to unionist hegemony in parliament.

The record shows that while in parliament between 1921-25, he was passionate about the building and allocation of houses for the people of Belfast city. As a businessman and Corporation member, the valuation of property in the city was a concern for him. He complained that the 1923 Housing Bill was inadequate and would fail to deliver the necessary housing. In early 1924, he asserted Belfast needed 5,000 new homes and he was apprehensive about how this might be achieved. During the final year of the parliamentary term, when he raised the matter in the commons, he drew groans from fellow politicians – 'Not again, Crawford'. It was this extraordinary passion and focus by McCullagh on housing in Belfast and the overt sincerity and commitment to the delivery of houses for the working class that contrasted deeply with what an official inquiry in 1926 revealed: that, to

---

[185] R. J. Lawrence, *The Government of Northern Ireland: Public finance and Public services* (Oxford, 1965). P. 62.

the public at large, there may have been a Machiavellian or wholly self-interest intent in McCullagh's concern about the delivery of housing in the city.

McCullagh was elected to the first parliament on 24 May 1921, polling 5,068 first preferences, and he was one of four members in the constituency of Belfast South. Polling in the general election for the second parliament on 3 April 1925 saw McCullagh coming bottom of the poll and he failed to keep his seat.[186] This was an immense disappointment to him and his fall from grace was linked to widespread rumours of gross maladministration in the Corporation over the provision of housing in the city.

In the first parliament, McCullagh had a profile of being a vigorous advocate of housing provision in the city and played a prominent role in implementing the Local Government Act (Ireland) in 1919, which obliged the Corporation to prepare its housing scheme. A housing committee of 15 members was established, with McCullagh as chairperson and T E McConnell as vice-chairperson. McConnell's family were wealthy estate agents in the city. The housing committee operated out of the City Solicitor's office and had a staff of valuers and agents. This committee devised a house-building scheme that involved constructing houses mainly by direct labour. The total number of houses erected by the corporation in the period 1919 and 1939 came to 2,562, and they built most of these before 1930.

The Corporation scheme progressed without wrangling until March 1925, when it emerged that officials purchased

---

[186] Brian Walker (ed.), *Parliamentary Election Results in Ireland, 1918-92*, pp. 45-47.

building materials without going to tender as required by law. The Corporation initially appointed two independent accountants to investigate the matter, and they reported and identified glaring deficiencies in the quality and quantity of timber purchased, along with the revelation that the Corporation itself was paying, in one contract alone, 25 percent more than the market price. They also concluded that the problem was rampant across the system.

McCullagh's housing committee did not take kindly to these findings and, in fact, 'fought a rear-guard action against the report'.[187] Disturbed by these findings, the Corporation, initiated a commission of inquiry into the housing scheme in September 1925 and appointed Robert Megaw KC to conduct it; it extended over four months and the results were published a year later, in October 1926.

Megaw and McCullagh were no strangers to one another. Both had been elected as Unionist members in the first parliament in 1921 and Megaw became the Parliamentary Secretary to the Ministry of Home Affairs. He, like McCullagh, failed to keep his seat in 1925. Megaw would have been familiar with McCullagh's personality and pointedly observed that McCullagh, as chairperson of the Housing Committee, would have been 'pleased to think that he was the guiding spirit of a magnificently conducted work'.[188] He posited McCullagh was the actual and the nominal leader on the Housing Committee, and supplied any information when the policy was planned or approved.

---

[187] I. Budge and C. O'Leary, *Belfast: Approach to Crisis* (London, 1973), p. 146.

[188] R. D. Megaw, *Report of Enquiry into the Housing Schemes of the Belfast Corporation* (October, 1926), p. 122.

Megaw concluded that the deficient and devious work of the Housing Committee, as disclosed in the inquiry, was down to 'the lack of a wise and strong guiding head, who would have seen, from the commencement, that a consistent policy was adopted and followed, *regardless of private interests*' (author's italics). Megaw pointed to T. E. McConnell as having an enormous influence on how McCullagh conducted the housing committee. McConnell had indeed strong views on the delivery of housing in Belfast city. He had represented the Corporation at the Local Government Inquiries of 1919 and 1920. Yet, for some unexplained reason, he was not asked to give evidence at Megaw's Enquiry and Megaw himself considered his absence a deficit because if he had been there 'he could have filled in many gaps where Sir Crawford McCullagh's recollection failed'.[189]

The report was scathing about the operation of the housing scheme. It found a litany of negative findings and gross ineptitude by officials and officers about inadequate checking of accounts, the requisitioning of inferior materials, with failure to explain both the quality and quantity of building materials tendered. Other grave charges were the allocation of contracts without tender and, more damning still, some members and officials of the Housing Committee, including the city solicitor, had financial interests in the building sites themselves. The Megaw report highlighted that the allocation of sites for new houses weighed heavily in favour of 'profit to the vendor and not suitable for working class housing'. When a million bricks were delivered to one firm, only 66,000 were accounted for, resulting in a tale of

---

[189] R. D. Megaw, p. 126.

Belfast folklore suggesting that the vanishing bricks were used to build a cinema owned by a member of the Housing Committee.[190]

Megaw ended his report by identifying the 'disinclination of everyone concerned' to facilitate the inquiry. The Housing Committee gave him 'incomplete and misleading documents' that had been fraudulently changed with Housing Department minutes that had been 'astutely manipulated'.[191] Megaw was sympathetic about how the Housing Committee wanted to provide houses in the city with the least cost to the ratepayer, but, given their remit, there was a blatant lack of supervision and no settled policy on how this was to be achieved.

The inquiry found that McCullagh, as chairperson of the committee, had failed to give the leadership expected from a seasoned politician and former lord mayor. The Housing Committee failed to produce documents, and some members were unwilling to give testimony, and the report did not mince words about 'a quite unjustifiable air of complacency by the chairperson, Sir Crawford McCullagh'.[192]

Maladministration in the Corporation was rife, and the possibility of rectifying matters in the future hung in the balance. The city solicitor and surveyor resigned, and some people implicated in the housing contracts were prosecuted. Sir Crawford McCullagh survived as there was nothing to directly link him with the maladministration of the housing scheme.

The Government was uneasy with these developments and urged the then lord mayor, W. Turner, to set up a special

---

[190] I. Budge and C. O'Leary, *Belfast: Approach to Crisis* (London, 1973), p. 168.
[191] R. D. Megaw, p. 7.
[192] I. Budge and C. O'Leary, p. 147.

committee to examine how the administration of the corporation could be improved and updated. The services of a London accountant, Arthur Collins, were engaged to spearhead a committee of six to investigate the structures and functions currently in place in the corporation.

The Collins report concluded that there were too many committees and that corporation members were interfering with work that should be the sole domain of officials, such as the hiring and firing of staff. It was a failure by Corporation members to distinguish between operational matters as opposed to their proper function, which was that of governance. The Collins report made over 30 recommendations based on how the Birmingham borough in the UK organized itself. This included the recommendation that the committee system be simplified and the introduction of a competitive system for appointments. The Corporation accepted all the recommendations and became law in 1930.

Consequent to this, there followed a dip in Crawford McCullagh's fortunes. In the local elections in 1929, when McCullagh stood for his Cromac seat in the corporation, W. H. Alexander, an independent Unionist and a leading manufacturer and member of the reform group in the Belfast Chamber of Commerce, stood against him. Alexander's campaign introduced the catchphrase 'immediate reforms or commissioners' (to run the Corporation).

As chairperson for the shamed housing committee, McCullagh had to take the blame for the 1926 fiasco report, and Alexander defeated McCullagh for the Cromac seat.[193] McConnell, the estate agent and McCullagh's vice-

---

[193] *Belfast Newsletter*, 16 January 1931.

chairperson, was also opposed in the local elections, but he got his opponent to withdraw. McCullagh, always resilient, bounced back and stood for the vacant council seat in Woodvale in 1930 and was elected.

Fortune again favoured him when William Coates retired as lord mayor and the councillors elected McCullagh to succeed him in 1931. During the 1930s, the Corporation itself faded from public controversy as more immediate matters became the focus of public concern. These were the riots in 1932 and 1935 over the failure of the Belfast Board of Guardians to live up to their responsibilities.

# 6

# CRAWFORD McCULLAGH IN THE SENATE 1931-1946

*All political lives, unless they are cut off in midstream at a happy juncture, end in failure, because that is the nature of politics and of human affairs.*

Enoch Powell MP

In City Hall during the 1930s, Sir Crawford McCullagh, who had been lord mayor during the Great War, the high-profile businessman and member of the first Northern Ireland parliament supervised, guided and directed a coterie of prosperous members of the business and professional classes in Belfast Corporation.

During his time, the first municipal aerodrome in the UK was built on Malone Road, and the Corporation Gas Department, by 1928, maintained the city's street lighting and produced more gas than the original Belfast Gas Light Company had produced in a year. McCullagh boasted that the price of gas to the consumer was the lowest in the UK even though the profits from the Gas Department subsidised the rates, electricity and the maintenance of the parks, libraries and public baths. The gas profits also contributed to the cost of building City Hall in 1906.[194]

The Corporation spent £3 million in the 1920s on the reconstruction of Belfast. Many roads were widened and

---

[194] J. Bardon, *Belfast, an illustrated history* (Belfast, 1982), p.205.

resurfaced, including the Malone Road, the Shankill Road, and the Falls Road. A bridge over the railway was built at Tates Avenue while the North Road Bridge was widened and a lock and weir constructed above the Albert Bridge. Despite this economic spend, the city councillors were preoccupied with keeping the rates down at all costs and subsequently little effort was made to address public health and corporation housing.

## In the Senate

Crawford McCullagh became a member of the Northern Ireland Senate six years after he failed to be re-elected to the Northern Ireland parliament in 1925. The Senate was the Upper House in the new Northern Ireland parliament and its function was expected to replicate similar work to that of the Upper House (the House of Lords) at Westminster.

Under the Government of Ireland Act (1920), the lord mayors of Belfast and Londonderry sat as ex officio senators, and remained senators so long as they were returned as lord mayor of their respective cities. The role of the lord mayor in the Senate went unnoticed until P. F. McGill's full-length study of the Northern Ireland Senate (1921-62). McGill was scathing of the contribution of the lord mayors of Belfast and Londonderry to Senate discussion and debates. He described their contribution as an 'apathetic discharge of their senatorial duties'. [195] He found that ex officio senators, such as the lord mayors of Belfast and Londonderry in the 1930s and 1940s,

---

[195] P. F. McGill, 'The Senate in Northern Ireland, 1921-1962' (Ph.D. thesis, Queen's University, Belfast, 1965), p. 254.

attended the Senate with 'modest regularity' and they had a reputation for gross absenteeism by the end of the Second World War.

During the 1930s, the ex officio senators were 'at their unobtrusive best' where poor attendance was correspondingly matched by lethargy in senate debates.[196] McGill recorded that the work in the Senate chamber confined itself largely to proposing or seconding the address-in-reply to the King's speech, and the occasional question or the 'rare event—participation in general debate.'[197]

In mitigation of this absenteeism by the lord mayors, it has been argued that 'the relations between the two urban corporations and the Government had been regulated in the normal way by official correspondence and discussion, and by deputations to ministers rather than by discussion on the floor of the Senate'.[198] In other words, there was no need or expectation for the lord mayors to contribute when the Senate was in session. However, a sound argument could be made that those ex officio senators, because of their appointment, had a broader brief to deal with matters other than those affecting their immediate municipalities.

McCullagh, as Lord Mayor of Belfast, served in the Senate for fifteen years from 1931 to 1946. On the floor of the House, he exercised 'an almost complete silence' and 'a visitor to the Chamber might readily assume the existence of an unwritten law against ex officio senators taking part in the

---

[196] Ibid., p. 265.
[197] Ibid., p. 267.
[198] A. G. Donaldson, 'The Senate in N. I.' in Public Law (1958), pp. 135-154.

proceedings'.[199] McGill observed that 'this is all the more remarkable in that the ex officio senators were thoroughly experienced in local government and thus possessed primary knowledge of the public view on important matters. In this, they had a marked advantage over many of the elected senators, for some of whom membership of the House was their first public office'.[200]

McGill further concluded that 'the record of the ex officio members as a category couldn't be considered as other than unimpressive. In general, they had contributed nothing of weight to the Senate's work … men who in their cities had been able public representatives had not been a success in the Senate'.[201]

The failure of ex officio members in the Senate to make an impression may have had something to do with the calibre of individual lord mayors. Attendance in the first parliament (1921-1925) by ex officio members was poor, and from 1925 the infrequency continued even though the ex-officials represented the two largest urban areas in Northern Ireland that were experiencing mounting unemployment when the economic depression deepened in the 1930s. The learned professions never figured in the ex officio membership in the city councils, and there was never a representative from the ranks of the linen manufacturers, the shipbuilding industries or leading industries in general.[202]

Crawford McCullagh, coming from humble origins and possessing only a primary school education, became a leading

---

[199] McGill, p. 268.
[200] Ibid.
[201] Ibid., p. 271.
[202] Ibid., p. 259.

businessman in the city. He was elected a member of parliament in the first parliament and later, as Lord Mayor of Belfast, he enjoyed the longest term in office of an ex officio member of the Northern Ireland Senate. McCullagh was highly thought of and became a baronet in 1935. He was a member of the Northern Ireland Privy Council and he was one of two members who retired from office at 78 years of age.

## City unrest in the 1930s

The Wall Street crash of 1929 had a huge impact on Belfast. World trade contracted and raised import controls, curtailing Belfast's export markets through the 1930s. Almost 60% of the workforce in the province was in Belfast in 1932, and unemployment in shipping and engineering reached 64%.

The crisis saw the end of the shipbuilder 'wee yard' of Workman Clark, its operation closing in 1935. No luxury liners were launched out of the Belfast docks. Linen output collapsed in the 1930s and the 86,762 employed in the trade in 1924 was reduced to 61,000. When the Gold Standard was abandoned in 1931 and the pound sterling fell, the linen trade in Belfast experienced a new lease of life. Yet, despite this, poverty in the city was such that those who relied on outdoor relief from the city workhouse were on the verge of starvation.[203]

The mounting poverty crisis in the city brought the working-class people together in a chorus of protests, demanding that authorities should do something about the situation. They directed the focus of their anger towards the guardians of the workhouse. The board of the Belfast

---

[203] *Belfast News Letter*, 2 October 1932.

workhouse had 34 members, or guardians, who were elected by the city ratepayers from the local government districts. Most board members were middle-class property owners, mainly Unionist, many with ambitions to aspire to a seat in City Hall or even to seek a seat in the parliament itself.

The guardians, originally in the old town hall, had now moved to Glengall Street. Their understanding of the poor law was very much grounded in the original idea that lay behind the workhouse itself. In this, they viewed the workhouse as a place of last resort, a grey, sombre building of deterrence that segregated the sexes on their arrival there. The workhouse split up families when they arrived, offered a poor diet to its inmates, and imposed heavy manual work for those unlucky enough to be there.

The recession had deepened in Belfast in the early 1930s. By September 1932, there were 78,000 men unemployed, which amounted to 28% of the insured workforce, with many no longer having claims to state benefit. In desperation, many sought help from the city workhouse guardians. The guardians believed that their purpose was not to relieve 'chronic distress' and certainly not to take up the tab for the Government's responsibility, and inability, to provide work and employment for the able-bodied. In this, the Government allowed the guardians to follow their traditional approach and did not intervene lest in doing so the Government itself might indeed be held to account for failing to sustain employment for the poor and needy.

The guardians believed it was not their function to 'subsidise idleness' and rejected applications from young applicants who had large families and who 'had not worked and are apparently not anxious to work'.[204] The matter was further exacerbated in that 60% of the applicants were Roman Catholic. This drew the unfortunate comment from the workhouse chairperson, Lily Coleman, that whatever you thought about poor circumstances, there was 'no poverty under the blanket'. The focus of the guardians was to guard the rates rather than protect the poor, and when they gave relief, it was measly when compared to other UK cities.

On 3 October 1932, the workers of Belfast organised a torchlight protest meeting with 60,000 present. They met at the Custom House to protest at the levels of relief.[205] On the opening of the parliament on 11 October, a hunger march which had been banned under the Special Powers Act arrived at Stormont buildings. Later in the day, rioting erupted across the city in Catholic and Protestant areas, resulting in clashes with the police who opened fire on demonstrators, and two men died from bullet wounds.[206] The Government reacted by putting pressure on the Corporation and the board of guardians to immediately increase outdoor relief payments for the able-bodied poor.

It was a historic moment in time and much comment has been made of the cooperation between the Protestant and Catholic communities in 1932 and how they had stood together against a recalcitrant regime that failed to address their economic needs. Their togetherness did not last as religious prejudice and sectarian strife intervened when both

---

[204] B. Barton, *The Blitz, Belfast in the War Years* (Belfast, 1989), p. 19.
[205] P. Devlin, *Yes, we have no bananas: outdoor relief in Belfast 1920-1939* ( Belfast, 1981), pp.116-36.
[206] R. Hayburn, 'The police and the hunger marchers' in *International Review of Social History*, vol. 17, No 2 (1972), p. 627.

communities later pursued limited work opportunities.

Belfast then was a city of urban villages where people hesitated to venture beyond their own boundaries because of persistent sectarian prejudice that allowed factions to thrive and foment trouble. In this, the Church and political factions controlled all aspects of social life. By 1935, rising tensions erupted like a semi-dormant volcano as the traditional 12 July commemorations, which had been initially banned, were allowed to proceed. Rioting, arson and sniper activity ensued for three weeks in the Shankill and the Falls areas of the city. Eleven people died and 574 were injured. There were 37 cases of malicious damage and 173 arson attacks, making it 'the most ferocious eruption of civil unrest to occur in Northern Ireland since 1922'.[207] Localised curfews and increased police and army presence helped to restore order. During this period of unrest in the city, Crawford McCullagh was the lord mayor, but by design or otherwise, he appeared to have very little role in quelling or restoring order in the events of 1932 and 1935.

In March 1932, McCullagh heralded the King's speech at the start of the fourth session of the Third Parliament.[208] The dominant theme of the speech related to economics and McCullagh's response ranged across several areas. He acknowledged that the industries of Northern Ireland had been given material assistance but observed that the call to reduce expenditure was a two-edged sword. With a substantial reduction in expenditure, the unemployment rate would increase across the province. He welcomed measures

---

[207] J.R. Hill, *A history of Ireland vol. vii*, 1921-1984, p. 214.
[208] The King's speech was read by a representative of the Crown, in this case, Viscount Aberdeen.

that were intended to reform a presently antiquated system of local government and agreed that reform was needed.

McCullagh supported rent restriction for smaller types of houses and he welcomed the subsidy for working-class dwellings. He regretted private builders had not entered the housing market and that the housing supply did not match demand. It particularly pleased him that the Corporation's electricity undertaking had proved to be an important factor in assisting the Government in its scheme of comprehensive electricity development.[209] When he finished his address, a fellow senator openly remarked that the voice of the lord mayor was too seldom heard in the House and when he spoke, his words were valued highly.[210]

It was another year before McCullagh rose to speak in the Senate. He continued to be concerned about the provision of housing in the city and rejected the notion that there were any slums; he believed slum areas had been cleared and uninhabitable houses had been 'taken down'. Numerous streets contained small houses which could be removed, enabling three streets to form into two.[211]

What was important, in his view, was that the Corporation and the Government should provide houses at a price at which they could be rented for a reasonable sum. He agreed it was not possible to return to pre-war prices, but both authorities could produce houses within the reach of the working man and reduce unemployment.[212] When the Housing Bill was debated on 2 November 1933, he opposed an amendment that

---

[209] N.L.I., OPNI Senate, X1V, pp. 6-8.
[210] Ibid., p. 15.
[211] N.L.I., OPNI Senate, XV, p. 153.
[212] Ibid., p. 155.

sought a regulation that a 'house is constructed by recognized building trade operatives and by recognized builders'. McCullagh wanted to know what a recognized builder was,[213] and he argued that only big builders should be allowed to build; his fellow councillors agreed.[214]

In 1933, the new parliamentary building opened at Stormont. When senators moved into their new chamber in Stormont, they complained about the acoustics and McCullagh became concerned that the public might get the impression that the parliament building wasn't fit for purpose, despite the huge amount of money that had been spent on the new facility. He himself had no complaints about the acoustics as he had heard every word spoken on the opposite side of the House; he advised the members that they just needed to get used to the new chamber. He recalled that when Belfast Corporation got their new council chamber in 1906, they experienced similar difficulties. He admonished the members to have patience and to speak clearly and distinctly.[215]

The following year, in June 1934, McCullagh found fault with the Finance Bill and took issue with the Government, observing that it had placed an unfair burden on the Corporation, demanding it struck a rate of 6d in the pound. He argued Belfast was under pressure to 'pay up' all the time while the city itself was under-resourced. He cited the example of schools. The most recent report from the Ministry of Education showed Belfast had only 209 elementary schools out of 1,837 across the province.

---

213 Ibid., pp. 475-6.
214 Ibid., pp. 484.
215 Ibid., p. 85.

## Motor car enthusiast

McCullagh was one of Belfast's first motorists and he bought his first car in 1903 from the Cuba Street works of the Chamber Brothers. His son, 'Boysie', and himself were car enthusiasts and purchased many models – a Darrig V14, an Alvis, an Austin, a Bentley and a Rolls Royce, and this passion was one of the few recreations McCullagh allowed himself.

McCullagh's interest in cars prompted him to question the amount of motor tax collected by the Government and how money was distributed with grants from a Road Fund. In June 1934, Belfast received £746,702 from the fund, while the rest of the province received over £4 million. Yet 40% of cars were registered in Belfast and, while they were not limited to the streets of Belfast, 75 – 80% percent of the annual expenditure on maintenance and improvement on roads was incurred by local authorities other than Belfast.[216] McCullagh did not think this was a fair distribution of funds.

McCullagh also had a view on speed limits in the city. When he was an MP back in the first Northern Ireland parliament, he thought people worried themselves too much about motor speed. In Ulster, a heavy motor car without a trailer was permitted to travel at 12 miles an hour only if the vehicle had pneumatic tyres and only if the registered axle weight did not exceed six tons. Otherwise, the motor was only permitted to travel 8 miles an hour. There was a concern abroad that a speed of 3 miles an hour in Donegal Place might be too much for the area. McCullagh's view was more pragmatic, and he was at pains to point out that the permitted

---

[216] N.L.I., OPNI Senate, XV1, pp. 291-292.

speed limit in England was 20 miles per hour.[217]

## Local Government Bill

On 30 October 1934, during the second reading of the Local Government Bill, McCullagh supported the major thrust of the provisions, though he considered the Bill did not go far enough in attempting to update out-of-date legislation. He particularly approved that the Bill did away with the stipulation that the lord mayor and the town clerk were required to go around and examine the city boundaries once a year: he certainly didn't 'fancy going to the slopes of the Cave Hill and then to Stormont to examine the boundaries'.

Seventeen months elapsed before McCullagh delivered his most acute criticism of the Government when, as lord mayor and leader of the city, he expressed concern that the relationship between the Government and the Corporation was not in a good place and nobody regretted this more than he did.

It was true the relationship was far from what it ought to be. There were frequent misunderstandings between the two bodies, and the root cause came from the financing of public services for which both the Government and the Corporation were responsible. There were no consistent principles of procedure in the financing of semi-national services. Each case was settled by expediency – a block grant, adopted by the Government to get them out of a hole, with no forward-thinking or planning.[218]

---

[217] Stormontpapers.ahds.ac.uk (accessed 21 April 2020), 4, p. 1116.
[218] N.L.I., OPNI Senate, XV111, pp. 163-167.

## Derating

A continual bugbear for McCullagh in the Senate was the question of derating on property. Belfast contributed more than half the taxes that were paid in Northern Ireland and these taxes formed the foundation of the Government's revenue, out of which the derating scheme was financed. Belfast, he argued, bore the brunt of the derating scheme. The agricultural property was derated and exempted from the Revaluation Act. McCullagh was opposed to any derating scheme. He had friends who disagreed with him as they owned land and others whose businesses made huge profits and paid no rates. McCullagh argued that, with the derating system, Belfast Corporation lost money that would not be recovered from the Government. The matter had caused 'a certain amount of ill-feeling' between the two bodies.

In 1938, in the debate on the King's speech, he expressed definite views on emigration. He had recently attended a conference in Mansion House in London at which there was a call on the Government to export surplus population to the colonies, where they were required, when they failed to find work at home. The Northern Ireland Government had already done valuable work in relocating people to work on the land in Canada. They had set committees up to do this and received the full support of the Imperial Government.

In the same debate, McCullagh expressed positive views on the value of lower taxation for businesses, especially new businesses. He cautioned that new business ought to grow slowly and firms should not be over-eager to expand before it was time.

McCullagh cited the case of the Dunlop Rubber Company

as the greatest industry of its kind in the world. When Dunlop patented their tyre in Belfast, he failed to appreciate the potential and refused the opportunity to invite the Rubber Company to the city. It was a missed opportunity and if Belfast had opened its door to Dunlop, the city would have played host and reaped the benefits from one of the greatest industries in the world. McCullough had recently been in the Dunlop factory premises and made overtures to them to come to Belfast. He believed that the best way to get a new industry was not to start from scratch but to entice an established business from the United Kingdom to open up in Belfast.

In May 1938, McCullagh was concerned about a clause in the Physical Training Bill that proposed to give the public the right to cross private lands to get to their place of recreation. McCullagh took grave exception to the possibility that it might be voted into legislation; he thought it an extraordinary power of access to give to anyone, a power which would allow people to go in and out as they liked on any man's private property to get to a bathing place or any other place of recreation.

He told the Senate that on a Sunday morning he experienced great difficulty keeping people off his residential land at his home in Lismara. He further objected to another clause in the Bill that would allow the Government to compulsorily take ground from an individual to build a recreational facility. He argued that such a land grab wasn't the same thing as a scheme to build new houses or new roads. Most people would give temporary accommodation for playing fields if it was sought, but not for their land to be arbitrarily taken.[219] McCullagh was suitably pleased when the offending clause was subsequently rescinded.

## Revaluation of property

Later in 1938, McCullagh expressed his delight that a newly appointed committee would examine the entire process of revaluation of property and the rating system. In his view, the whole business of re-evaluation was one of the worst things that ever happened in the city, as nobody had considered that there would be far-reaching effects. It was a shock for many to realize that in the revaluation process, an increase of 45% was anticipated. He was all for tidying up and removing anomalies, but the high rise in rates was a major blow to business in a time of depression.

One aim of the valuation was to raise money through taxation to run the country. When appeals were made, there was little reduction in valuations. The hardest treatment had been experienced by shopkeepers. When McCullagh walked down York Street from Donegal Street, he could count 21 vacant shops because of high valuation. On the other hand, the Government would pay over £112,000 a year to wealthy concerns who made huge profits and paid huge dividends. He called on the Government to bring in a Bill immediately that would deliver some relief, not just to Belfast but to the province itself.[220]

On the eve of the Second World War, McCullagh was concerned that people from Northern Ireland had to get a

---

[219] N.L.I., OPNI Senate, XX1, p. 220.
[220] Ibid., p. 334-336.

permit to cross over to England and that it took ten days to get a permit. He thought the ten-day wait was ridiculous and cited an example of a lady on holiday in Northern Ireland who wished to return home to the UK but was told by the police that she would have to wait ten days. McCullagh intervened, and she had her permit that day. In a Senate debate, the incident drew a strong rebuke from Major Dobbs, who objected sharply to McCullagh's anecdote as 'the use of what is called backstairs influence'. It wasn't right that someone who applied to the lord mayor could obtain a permit in one day, while others had to wait ten days.

In late September 1939, with the threat of war looming, McCullagh was in favour of setting up a system of air-raid warders and shelters. Unlike others, McCullagh believed Belfast was in danger from German air raids. He pointed out that Belfast was mentioned in German broadcasts every week and believed precautions should be taken. Others seemed to think there would be no war and no air raids on Belfast. However, the lord mayor failed to energise fellow councillors in the Corporation to seriously consider adequate precautions and to have air raid shelters built in the city environs.[221]

During 1940, McCullagh had little engagement with the Senate other than to pay tribute to Lord Craigavon on his death in November, and earlier when he urged the Government to go step-by-step in everything with the imperial authorities.[222] In October 1941, McCullagh was in attendance at the Senate when a ministerial question revealed a shortage of matches in Northern Ireland. This particularly

---

[221] Ibid., p. 340.
[222] N.L.I., OPNI Senate, XX111, p. 279.

interested McCullagh, who was a director of Messrs Maguire and Patterson, a supplier of matches to the city. He informed the Senate that his company had large supplies, but the match trade was entirely under the Board of Trade in Manchester and the Control Office in London. Deliveries could only be made under license and customers' orders had to be submitted directly to the Match Control Office for approval and delivery. There was the same shortage in London as in Belfast.

In May 1942, a new lord mayor of Belfast, George Ruddell Black, was sworn in. However, he died six months later on 28 December and, on 6 January 1943, McCullagh was again elected to the role. Back in office, with the popular support of his fellow councillors, he engaged with the debate on the King's speech with renewed vigour.

The King's speech in the Belfast parliament was upbeat. It called for more volunteers for the war effort and a greater effort from the farming community. Input from the shipbuilding, engineering and textile industries had increased. Unemployment was down and large numbers of women were engaged in the munition factories. Auxiliary electricity plants were in place to meet any emergency.

Despite the societal controversy surrounding conscription, McCullagh demanded that it should be enforced in Northern Ireland.

Again, with a reference to derating, his bug-bear, he was especially pleased that the Government was concerned about the effect of derating on social developments and that it was proposing to bring forward legislation to help the authorities to carry out essential improvements to the derating system. As a businessman, McCullagh believed that in times of depression, industries could be helped by a system of derating, but when the economy picked up it ought to cease. He declared it was the 'little man' who should readily gain in any derating system and the transfer should come from wealthy firms to struggling traders.

## Housing again

As he came to the end of his term as lord mayor, the Belfast housing question was never far from his thoughts. He admonished the members of parliament about their confused and mixed-up thinking surrounding the building of new houses and the over-charging of rents. House prices were way beyond what people could afford to pay and he considered that one of the 'greatest evils' of the time was the practice of people with money investing in houses and then sub-letting them out as rooms or flats.

McCullagh believed that the present Planning Bill did not properly address the business of rebuilding in the city. The Government needed to be proactive, as neither private enterprise nor the Corporation could build. There was a shortage of materials and there were restrictions on the amount one could spend on rebuilding. There were presently 5,000 people on a waiting list for corporation housing and while he supported the Planning Bill for the city because it wouldn't do any harm, 'it certainly does not do much good'.[223]

For McCullagh, the Corporation's problem was the difficulty of acquiring land to build new houses. Houses had been demolished and there were vacant spaces all over the city, yet it appeared that there was not sufficient ground

---

[223] N.L.I., OPNI Senate, XXV1, p. 234.

within the present city boundaries. Individuals had already moved out of the city to avoid paying rates while still availing of all the amenities that the city offered – gas, electric light, transport. An individual could earn his living in the city, but by residing outside, he escaped all his responsibilities.

For McCullagh, the Planning Commission and the authorities needed to engage together to agree on the development of the city and to acquire additional land in the surrounding districts.[224] In January 1944, he acknowledged that a planning scheme for any authority was a bigger job than most people realized. It took months and months to acquire information and, in this regard, he thought there should be no time limit on the current planning bill. His advice was taken.[225]


## Community role

Outside of his role in the Senate, McCullagh played a leading part in Belfast's life during the 1930s. In March 1935, he was invited to do a radio series on the history of Belfast, which turned out to be very popular with the city's citizens. In 1936, he had been lord mayor for six years in succession, and he helped his son, Joseph Crawford, McCullagh to get a seat on the city council representing Clifton district. After an initial bout of enthusiasm, the young McCullagh dropped out of sight and rarely attended Corporation meetings.

Despite the Depression of the 1930s there were significant municipal developments in the city that allowed McCullagh to

---

[224] Ibid., p. 454.
[225] N.L.I., OPNI Senate, XXV1, pp. 475-479.

exercise his role as lord mayor. The five volumes of family press clipping in the Governor's Room in the Linen Hall Library in Belfast point to a man who enjoyed every ceremonial occasion.

When a new Belfast mental hospital was opened in 1935 and a new firefighting station in 1936, McCullagh was there. He opened the new Boyne Bridge in December 1936 on the site of Belfast's oldest bridge constructed in 1717. The administration and organisation of educational facilities in the city came under the remit of the Corporation following the Education Act of 1923. The Corporation's Education Committee was obliged to build, organise and enlarge elementary schools, and McCullagh opened one or two schools a year.

In 1935, the Corporation found it fit to challenge the new Finance Act (NI) which required local authorities to levy an education rate to pay for services. Members were very sensitive to anything to do with city rates and McCullagh himself challenged the validity of the act, suggesting that imposing the levy was income tax by another name which only the imperial parliament had the authority to impose, according to the Government of Ireland Act 1920. The matter went to a judicial review, and the Corporation lost its plea and reluctantly accepted the new levy.[226]

The late 1930s were good for Belfast, with a great impetus given to engineering and building. In 1935, Harland and Wolff recorded the highest ship tonnage in the world, and three years later it boasted the largest shipping output in the

---

[226] I. Budge and C. O'Leary, *Belfast: approach to crisis* (London, 1973), p. 152.

United Kingdom. The secret of its success lay in the yard's ability to diversify its product. They built the first diesel-electric trams in the British Isles, supplied conventional locomotives for North and South America, engineered oil pipelines, and fabricated steel structures for shops and entertainment venues such as cinemas.

Elsewhere, the aircraft factory of Short and Harland experienced huge success in developing land and marine aircraft. In the inter-war years, economic conditions thrived across the province with 70 - 80% of the insured workforce at work. As a measure of prosperity, private cars on the roads increased tenfold between 1919 and 1937. More people took up golf and leisure activities, such as yachting, and people flocked to Ravenhill to watch rugby internationals.

Wireless communications took a quantum leap in Ulster when the BBC established a transmitter in 1924 and half of the population had a wireless set on the eve of the Second World War. There was a telephone exchange hub in the city and households were actively encouraged to avail themselves of electricity supply. In Belfast, McCullagh was at the centre of all these new initiatives. In personality, he enjoyed being a great publicist and deliverer of services.

He attended the opening of the first civil airport at Newtownards on 31 August 1934; in May 1935, he turned on the floodlights at City Hall and he hosted the trolleybus system in 1938. Press cuttings show him driving the last tramway car on the Falls Road on 30 April 1938. When the Ulster Development Council was set up in 1938 to promote Northern Ireland as an industrial base, McCullagh, as lord mayor, officiated at all major inaugural openings of new developments.

The Daily Express described him at the time as 'bluff, cheery, and of a domineering personality, he infuses the mayoralty with a warm friendliness than enhances rather than diminishes the office of Chief Citizen. He entertains liberally, so lavishly that Belfast is noted and admired the world over for its civic hospitality.'[227]

## Assessing McCullagh's role in the Senate

In assessing the role of the Senate in the Northern Ireland parliament, P. F. McGill deduced that the Senate had members of 'marked capacity' who were competent and able to deliver.[228] Yet, in McCullagh's time, the Senate's achievement had 'not been outstanding' and '[the Senate] must be regarded as having failed in its duty as a revising chamber'.[229] McGill considered that matters of importance were hurried through the Senate with little or no debate – simply rubber-stamped and passed. The abstention rate by ex officio members (the lord mayors) had 'not even been faintly justified'.[230] McGill suggested that a criticism made of the House of Lords might aptly apply to the Northern Ireland Senate: 'it represents no interests save the well sited camps of the party politicians and exists as an institution almost unknown to the mass of the community; it has achieved nothing that would make it remembered were it to vanish tomorrow.'[231]

The first substantial reference to McCullagh in the Senate

---

[227] Cunningham, p. 246.
[228] P. F. McGill, p. 400.
[229] Ibid.
[230] McGill, p. 401.
[231] Ibid., p. 404.

came in December 1931 when he exercised a concern, and not for the first time, on the quality control of milk coming into the city from outside sources. His contribution to debates in the early 1930s was slight as he was still under a cloud after the housing fiasco of the late 1920s when he was considered to be the main protagonist in a shady property scheme.

Over the years, his contributions in the Senate were relatively few and confined to matters on housing, emigration, city rates and the loss of business opportunities, as exemplified in the failure to attract the Dunlop Rubber Company to Belfast. He aired his issues when he voiced concern about people trespassing on his land. The contentious issue of property valuation (he had been at one time the biggest ratepayer in the city) was a personal bug-bear of his. He had a passing consideration in house planning, a concern about permits to England in wartime, and what could be done about the shortage of matches (as already stated, he was a director of the match supplier Messrs Maguire and Patterson).

In reply to the King's Speech in the mid-1940s, when he was 76 years old, he focused on 'old reliables' –conscription, labour disputes, derating, illegal organisations and social security issues. None of these topics were explored in any depth other than receiving a glossary mention, and in this, it probably reflected on his overall contribution to both his time in the first Northern Ireland parliament and his later time in the Senate.

## The Whiteabbey scandal

In 1941, towards the end of his time as lord mayor, another huge scandal (on a par with the housing scandal in the 1920s) engulfed the Corporation. This time (unlike the housing scandal), McCullagh was exonerated of any personal wrongdoing, but there is no doubt he suffered huge reputational damage as lord mayor of the city.

The corporation had been responsible for the maintenance and the oversight of Whiteabbey Sanatorium when, in 1941, deep unrest erupted among the staff. The Government, mindful of past Corporation ineptitude and mismanagement, initiated an inquiry into the entire administration of the hospital. John Dunlop, a ministry inspector, led the investigation. Shades of the Megaw inquiry, sixteen years previously, emerged when the Corporation decided not to facilitate the inquiry and instructed that evidential material should be withheld. The inquiry sat for 34 days and issued a report on 15 June 1941.

The inquiry found against the Corporation's treasury department, citing 'complete laxity' and 'gross neglect' in the management of accounts. The report revealed that the tuberculosis committee had attempted to purchase a site for the sanatorium with no regard for its suitability and a purchase price that was blatantly exorbitant. The report found that 'totally unsuitable' blackout material was sourced and purchased to supposedly prevent German bombers targeting them at night. Dunlop recommended that the tuberculosis committee should be dissolved and that the Corporation should be relieved of its powers under the

Tuberculosis Prevention Act.[232]

McCullagh, having experienced the fall-out from the maladministration of the Corporation housing scheme in the late 1920s, was very keen to engage with the Dunlop report positively but not all councillors were of the same frame of mind. As lord mayor and the leader of the city, he participated in the formation of a high-powered committee to engage with the issues raised in the inquiry.

First, the committee resolved to control future appointments to the sanatorium and traced the faulty blackout material to an industrial firm in which four current Corporation councillors had a vested interest. When the committee reported to a Corporation meeting on 7 August 1941, the immediate response was to 'shoot the messenger' and members voted to ignore the lord mayor and dissolve the committee.

Frantic 'behind the scenes' meetings took place over the next week and when the Corporation reconvened a week later, McCullagh had the original vote reversed and the committee was allowed to continue their work. A new town clerk was appointed and a return to the direct contract employment of semi-skilled and unskilled workers was recommended, and a 'conflict of interest' roll-call for council members was put in place.

The following April 1942, the total recommendations of the committee came before the Corporation for ratification. Members rejected all recommendations by a vote of eighteen to fourteen. McCullagh was no longer the lord mayor and, when in his mayoral role, he had failed to deliver much-

---

[232] Dunlop Report, p. 43.

needed reforms. Considering this, the Government appointed three administrators to oversee the administration of the city for a three-and-a-half-year period. The task of the administrators was to ensure that all the appointees in City Hall oversaw purchases, contracts, rates and municipal taxes. The then lord mayor, G. R. Black, after nine months in office, died in December 1942 and Corporation members once again turned to McCullagh and re-elected him lord mayor. With the Corporation now in administration, the mayoralty was a titular office and McCullagh remained there until 1946.

In his report, John Dunlop exonerated McCullagh for having done his best to implement reform before the Corporation went into administration. He described McCullagh's 'fearless and impartial leadership of the best elements in the council' and there was no mention of his inability to control wayward councillors and deliver reform.

# 7

# A TALE OF TWO LORD MAYORS

*Either one lives 'for' politics or one lives 'off' politics.*
Max Weber

*I have done the state some service, and they know't.*
*No more of that.*
Othello (Act v, Sc. 2)

Alfie Byrne and Crawford McCullagh came from humble
origins. Byrne was born on the 14th March 1882, the second
of eight children, at 36 Seville Place, Dublin, in a five-roomed
terraced house. The streets around were described as 'long
haggard corridors of rottenness and ruin'. His father Tom
Byrne worked in Dublin port at a plethora of jobs ranging
from ship's engineer, docker, engine fitter, ship's pilot. He
lost his job in the port in 1895 because he was over-ambitious
in seeking increased pay and better working conditions.

With Byrne out of work, the family downsized their home
to a smaller two-bed dwelling at 28 Lower Oriel Street. To
make ends meet at home, Alfie and his brother had to leave
school and Alfie became an apprentice in a bicycle shop in
Dawson Street; in the evenings, he sold programmes outside
the Tivoli Theatre on Burgh Quay. His interest in biking never
left him and, in later life, he cycled everywhere in the city. In
contrast, McCullagh was fascinated by the motor car in which
he maintained a lifelong interest that he passed on to his son,
Crawford Junior. McCullagh's early career, like Byrne's, also

took the route of an apprenticeship when he arrived in Belfast in 1882 and, like Byrne, supplemented his income by selling newspapers after work.

Apprenticeships were an important entrée into the world of work throughout the nineteenth century as it was the most important formal method for training skilled workers in all forms of business.[233] Most apprenticeships lasted approximately seven years, and this was reflected in the time McCullagh spent in the Bank Buildings in Belfast.[234]

In 1901, Byrne's father became re-employed in the Dublin docks and Alfie worked as a barman near the family home. The owner of the pub, Tom Heagney, an Offaly man, took a particular interest in the young Dubliner's progress.

It was here in the convivial pub surroundings that Byrne discovered he had a knack for dealing with many people. He learned the art of listening to people and acquired skills that allowed him to understand what made people 'tick'. Similarly, McCullagh's experience in the Bank Buildings in Belfast, as he attended to the needs of all types of customers, prepared him well for a political role later in life. The pub owner, Tom Heagney became a mentor to Byrne and played a similar role to that of William Gibson in the life of Crawford McCullagh.

Ambitious to progress in the pub trade, Byrne moved jobs to manage a pub called Cosgroves on Chancery Place beside the Four Courts. It was there that he noticed that members of the Irish Parliamentary Party had close associations with the liquor and public house trade. Byrne discovered that contacts

---

[233] L. Calvert, 'Apprenticeship, Adolescence and Growing Up in eighteenth - and nineteenth-century Ulster', in *Irish Economic and Social History, XLV* (2018), p.71.
[234] Ibid., p.70.

with the IPP augured well for his political aspirations.

Parnell had died in 1890, but in 1900, party members buried their differences under the new leadership of John Redmond. It was to be a new beginning and Byrne saw himself at the fore of political developments. Another potential power base that did not escape the young Byrne was the fact that half the members of the city council owned 89 tenements and second-class dwellings in the city and exercised a substantial say in how patronage was distributed throughout the community. Heagney encouraged Byrne's interest in politics and gave his blessing when Byrne married his only daughter, Cissie.

In 1908, Byrne purchased the Verdon Bar at 37 Talbot Street for a substantial sum of money, reportedly £500.[235] Like Crawford McCullagh in his early business ventures in Belfast, it was unclear how the money was raised. At 26 years of age, Byrne had no real money of his own, but no doubt his future father-in-law helped and the local branch of the United Irish League, where Byrne was the treasurer, may have helped to bankroll a political protégé.

There was a large representation of publicans on the city council who had political links to the Irish Party and they may have had a biased interest in furthering the career of a young political hopeful. In December 1910, the United Irish League selected Byrne as a candidate in the North Dock Ward, reputedly the largest working-class district in the country. On 16 January 1911, they elected him to the Dublin Corporation.[236] At 28 years old, it was to be the beginning of

---

235 *Sunday Chronicle*, 22 September 1937.
236 T. White, *Alfie Byrne* (Dublin, 2017), p. 8.

a long and memorable political career. Five years previously, in 1906, Crawford McCullagh had taken his seat in Belfast Corporation.

Both Crawford McCullagh and Alfie Byrne were full of enthusiasm when they arrived at their respective councils. They signed up for numerous committee projects, with McCullagh in particular becoming the chair of various committees. Byrne's youthful enthusiasm knew no bounds; he joined eleven committees across a host of concerns – housing, water, sanitation, public health, the Dublin Port and Docks Board, and the Poor Law Union.[237] Such was his commitment, he was seldom at home.[238]

In an interview with the *Daily Express* newspaper, he revealed the greatest number of functions he had attended in one day was 31, 'including meetings, dinners, and dances'.[239] He had no role in the Dublin lockout in 1913 other than spirited attempts on his part to have workers re-employed when the lockout was over.[240] He also protested against the suggestion at the time that Dublin children should be sent over to England for their safekeeping when the Dublin lockout was at its zenith.

Big Jim Larkin, the Labour leader, and Byrne portrayed themselves as saviours of the Dublin poor and over the years canvassed the same vote. Larkin, the outsider, had most to fear from Byrne and was vociferous in his contempt for the Dubliner.

---

[237] D. McEllin, 'Legendary Lord Mayor Alfie Byrne' in R. McManus and L. Griffith (eds), *Leaders of the City* (Dublin, 1913), p. 153.
[238] White, P. 11.
[239] D. McEllin, p. 163.
[240] Ibid., P. 12.

Back then, pub premises in Dublin played a central role in canvassing for votes in city elections, and Larkin had no problem labelling Byrnes's pub as a 'sink of political and other corruption'. It was the rendezvous of 'slum landlords, scabs, prostitutes, bullies . . . Hibs, Orangemen, Temperance humbugs . . . the brothel keeper, the white slaver'. [241]Larkin's tirade had little effect on Byrne's growing popularity as he proved himself to be a natural canvasser, committed to resolving problems for all. When elected, Byrne topped the poll and retained the title of alderman for the next ten years.

Though never a natural canvasser like Alfie Byrne, Crawford McCullagh's high point as lord mayor came during the First World War when, as leader of the city, he was ably supported in his mayoral functions by his wife, the lady mayoress. When McCullagh became lord mayor of Belfast for the first time in 1914, he already had a considerable high profile in the Belfast business community, and throughout the war years, his business interests in the city had continued to thrive.

Always ambitious, Byrne, in October 1914, made it known that he aspired to become lord mayor of Dublin, but he failed to get the support of fellow council members. Alderman John Clancy was elected, but before they could inaugurate him, he died suddenly. Byrne thought that because of his original interest in the position of lord mayor he had an excellent opportunity to succeed him. However, the councillors opted for someone else.

In the same year, Crawford McCullagh, with the support

---

[241] *Irish Worker*, 17 January 1914, quoted by Padraig Yeates in *A city in wartime, Dublin 1914-18* (Dublin, 2012), p. 62.

of the influential businessman, Otto Jaffé, was elected lord mayor of Belfast on the death of the sitting incumbent. In Dublin, Byrne, having failed to rally support from fellow councillors to become lord mayor, was undaunted. He now had a bigger target in his sights: the mother of all parliaments, Westminster itself.

McCullagh, unlike previous lord mayors of the city, never aspired to become a member of the Imperial Parliament to represent Belfast. A parliamentary seat was not an option when war broke out in 1914. He had to focus on his business interests and cope with the demands made during his time as lord mayor.

In contrast, failing to become lord mayor of Dublin in 1914 was a catalyst for Byrne's ambition. On the death of William Abraham MP, a member of the Irish Party, Byrne declared he would seek to run for the vacant seat. He had now sold his public house because, according to himself, it was a loss-making enterprise.

The parliamentary campaign ran for four weeks and, on 2 October 1915, Byrne emerged victorious, defeating two other nationalist candidates, and was duly elected as the new member of the Harbour Division of Dublin. Byrne was very pleased with the prospect of a parliamentary salary of £400 and he took to Westminster like the proverbial duck to water. At thirty-three, he was one of the youngest MPs in the Irish Parliamentary Party. He took his mandate from the Dublin docklands seriously and was often on the floor of the House of Commons, hassling the Home Secretary or the Chief Secretary for Ireland with a plethora of questions regarding factories in Ireland, army pensions, and such minutiae as the cost of tea and sugar. Unlike McCullagh, he was opposed to introducing conscription in Ireland.

## Easter 1916

Byrne was in Dublin during the 1916 Rising. He was opposed to it, as it cut across everything he believed in as a constitutional nationalist. As the insurrection progressed, he and the pacifist Francis Sheehy Skeffington combed the streets of Dublin, both wearing a white armband, urging Dubliners not to loot shops as chaos enveloped the city.

The rebels surrendered on 29 April with 485 people dead, 40 of them children. Sixteen leaders were executed by the army authorities and 1,800 rebels were transported to Frongoch in Wales and to other detention centres on mainland Britain. In the summer of 1916, Byrne crossed over to Wales to visit Frongoch, conscious that many of those detained there were his Dublin constituents.

He made a particular point of visiting women who had been interred for their rebel activities during the week of the Easter Rising. On one occasion, he entertained female prisoners at a local teashop, with two uniformed prison warders chaperoning. When the rebel Countess Markievicz was released from Aylesbury Prison at his invite, she came to tea on the terrace of the House of Commons.[242]

While McCullagh from very early in his career was a staunch member of the Unionist Party, Alfie Byrne never joined a political party after he lost his seat as a member of the Irish Party in 1918. In the local elections in January 1920, he overwhelmingly defeated the Sinn Fein candidate (3,180

---

[242] White, p. 27.

against 826). In the same year, he bought two large Victorian houses in Dartmouth Square for the sum of £1,200, triple the price he paid for his original pub investment, and he moved his family into one of them; he then sold the second house. Around the same time, along with five other men, he purchased several hundred acres of prime land at Kilmartin, Castleknock.[243]

The War of Independence between Ireland and England began in 1919 and ended in a truce; the Anglo-Irish Treaty was signed in 1921. It was not what most southern Irish people had hoped for, but it was deemed 'a stepping stone' to better things. The terms of the Treaty established an Irish Free State which was to be a dominion of the British Commonwealth. Members of a new Dublin parliament would take an oath of allegiance to the Crown and the six Ulster counties were free to opt-out of the Free State.

Not everyone agreed with the terms of the Anglo-Irish Treaty. Anti-Treaty forces gathered around De Valera and a vicious civil war broke out at the end of June 1922, and continued over ten months. On the pro-Treaty side were the Free State army forces. The conflict left Irish political society fractured, and not a little dysfunctional throughout the following 40 years. Byrne supported the Treaty from the beginning and they elected him as an Independent Nationalist for the Dublin mid constituency in 1922 and 1923.

Byrne had close affiliations with Cosgrave, the president of the Executive Council of Government after the deaths of Arthur Griffith and Michael Collins. Now, he found himself propelled to high office as lord mayor of Dublin *pro tem*, while

---

[243] Ibid., p. 33.

the incumbent, Lawrence O'Neill, was indisposed. Byrne and Cosgrave had a lot in common. They were both educated by the Christian Brothers and both had experience in the pub trade. Byrne, though not a party man, was to give his allegiance to Cosgrave's party over the next 30 years. In 1924, a corruption scandal arose in the allocation of houses in Dublin Corporation. It did not directly involve Byrne, but when he became lord mayor in 1930, he developed questionable affiliations with an English building society that arguably conflicted with his role as lord mayor.

The corruption scandal in Dublin was a red flare for the authorities in Belfast, who then initiated an inquiry into housing and unearthed a scandal that had Crawford McCullagh at its centre over the following two years. The Dublin Government's inquiry into the corruption there resulted in the suspension of Dublin Corporation for six years while a three-man commission oversaw the work of the Dublin Council.

In the meantime, Byrne's political rise continued. In the first two general elections in 1927, he topped the poll and secured more votes than anyone else in the country. The press summed it up: 'He is a party to himself. He has no organisation, no backing, no Big Noise to shout him along. During the campaign he made no speeches and fielded no meetings.'[244] Byrne's Dáil contributions were unremarkable and lacked the enthusiasm he showed when in the Westminster parliament. He railed against Ernest Bligh's cut in the old-age pension and decried partition as 'the greatest crime against the peace and prosperity of Ireland'.

---

[244] *Sunday Independent*, 12 June 1927.

## McCullagh in the NI Senate

A new parliament building to house both the Northern Ireland Commons and the Senate opened at Stormont in November 1932 (Fig.6).

6. Crowds gather for the opening of
Stormont Buildings 1932.

McCullagh attended the Northern Ireland Senate infrequently in the 1930s. A year could pass before he appeared in the chamber, and when he did attend there were recriminations by others that he seldom spoke. He did, however, appear when he considered that his own interests were under threat. In 1941, there was a shortage of matches and, as director of Messrs Maguire and Patterson, he assured parliamentary colleagues that the company had a reservoir of supply but that the Board of Trade held it up in London.

As the 1930s depression took hold in Belfast, he had a shadowy presence in conflict arenas. He played a minor role in the workhouse's resolution conflict in 1932 when the trade unions, unhappy with the Corporation's response to the Board of Guardians' outdoor relief measures, demanded that the Ministry of Home Affairs get involved.[245] When in 1935 the city experienced the worst rioting since 1922, the lord mayor appeared to have a minor role in quelling and restoring public order.

In 1928, Byrne made the momentous decision to retire from the Dáil and to run for election to the Irish Senate, Seanad Éireann. The rationale for this move was that it reduced the work of an elected representative in the Dáil while, as a member of the Senate, he still drew down a similar salary. He argued it would allow him the time to attend to the needs of his constituents.[246]

The composition of the Irish Senate comprised 60 senators, with 15 of them unattached to any party, and the independents 'were persons of the most diverse views, and the majority were men of distinction'.[247] The senators received the same allowance as Dáil deputies: £360 annually, with an allowance of £30 a month for unvouched expenses. It was alleged that the Senate met on average about 40 days in the year: 'for watching the Clerk stamp Government Bills and of discussing the advisability of adjourning for tea'.[248] Two-thirds of the senators attended regularly, but there was always a non-attendance scandal by the few, and the Senate in

---

[245] PRONI, LA/7/3/A/6.
[246] *Irish Independent*, 17 May 1928.
[247] D. O'Sullivan, *The Irish Free State and its Senate* (London, 1940), p. 268.
[248] Ibid., p. 512.

Northern Ireland had a similar experience.

The move to the Senate conveniently allowed Byrne to explore new avenues of personal enrichment that avoided the scrutiny he would be under as a public representative in the Dáil. The workload of senators then was relatively light and their public profile of no great significance.

In 1929, when Byrne was invited to become a trustee of the Royal Liver Friendly Society, the position provided Byrne with further income. It also gave him an entrée into people's lives where he could canvass for political support. In this, there may indeed have been a conflict of interest, but back then, a conflict of interest mattered less in a young fledgling state. Byrne resigned from the Senate in 1931 to make way for George Crosby of the *Cork Examiner* newspaper, who was a close ally of the Cosgrave party.

Dublin Corporation was prorogued in 1924 but was reconstituted in 1930 under a new act of parliament; its catchment area now extended to the independent townships of Pembroke, Rathgar and Rathmines. They appointed a city manager with a complement of staff spread across several departments: finance, public health, streets and water. The manager and staff would report to 35 elected Corporation members.

At the same time, an independent review sought the abolition of the office of lord mayor as an outdated and irrelevant function, but the recommendation was rejected. Removing Belfast's lord mayor never arose as an issue when the Corporation went into administration in the 1940s and McCullagh returned as lord mayor when its powers were restored.

## Lord Mayor again

Byrne's withdrawal from the senate allowed him to target the new, lucrative, paid position of the lord mayor of Dublin in the newly reconstituted Corporation in 1930. In the elections to the Corporation, he topped the poll and was elected to lead the city as lord mayor in October 1930. The *Evening Standard* heralded his elevation to the mayoralty as a 'rags to riches' story – a bicycle shop mechanic to be the First Citizen of the city.[249]

The *Belfast Telegraph*, which had seen many a lord mayor come and go, commented that 'everybody agrees that he is a decent sort, and all classes give him their votes. Generally he supports the Government; but he is not really much concerned with party politics'.[250] A year later when Byrne was re-elected as lord mayor, the paper appeared no wiser about the enigma of Byrne, describing him as 'a curious study, because apart from his public position he is an absolute nobody. He is unlearned – he is not a big businessman; he is not a politician'.[251]

Once elected, Byrne sold his own home and moved into the Mansion House on Dawson Street. It was a bold move suggestive of a man who considered himself in 'for the long haul'. The position came with the trappings of a secretary and a house steward. Byrne had more ambitious aspirations and saw the need to hire a second secretary and a chauffeur, along with the employment of three housemaids; this was all financed from his own pocket.

---

[249] White, P. 44.
[250] *Belfast Telegraph*, 18 October 1930.
[251] *Belfast Telegraph*, 4 July 1931.

In 1930, Dublin's lord mayor salary came to £2,500, making Byrne the highest-paid politician in the country. In his first year in office, he targeted young people and children as a way of obtaining the votes of their parents. It worked. He organised extravagant parties for children in the Mansion House and, when out and about, he carried sweeties and toffee bars on his person to distribute to children along the way.

Byrne had a huge capacity to ingratiate himself with people and was forever proffering his hand to all and sundry, gaining the appellation and reputation of being *The Shaking Hand of Dublin*.[252] He had the common touch and frequently travelled on public transport, chatting freely to people along the way. He was a workaholic. His work ethic was phenomenal; he accepted multiple invitations to dinners, plays and public functions. Politics was everything to him. He had no interests or hobbies other than to be available to the people of Dublin around the clock and his home was open day and night to all comers.

He undoubtedly had an instinct for the odd, mad escapade. When Clones town experienced a raging fire in December 1930, he donned firefighter clothes and rode there on the high seat of a Dublin fire brigade. On another occasion, he insisted on taking a test flight in Baldonnel against the advice of the airdrome staff , who felt that the weather was too unpredictable and dangerous. Byrne ignored the advice and when he returned to *terra firma,* declared to the press that 'air-mindedness was the thing of the future'.[253] Byrne had a penchant to be the first to appear at the scene of

---

[252] White, p. 50.
[253] *Evening Mail,* 7 September 1931.

any local disaster. On one occasion, when part of the city experienced flooding, he was out and about 'touring the land-hit areas, sympathising, organising, and encouraging'.[254]

As an elected representative, Byrne's focus was on 'bread and butter issues'. All politicians seek to show concern for their constituents in a myriad ways – housing, old-age pensions, hospital accommodation and business issues. Byrne had a huge daily postbag of petitions and requests. He worked around the clock and was never at home, though he had fathered eight children, with a track record of attending a multitude of events in a single day. Not being a populist politician in the same league as Alfie Byrne, McCullagh's postbag focused more on constituents hoping for a job in the Corporation itself.

## McCullagh's postbag

Most often the lord mayor' secretary responded to constituents, and McCullagh was at pains to point out that Corporation regulations stated that semi-skilled or unskilled workmen had to be recruited through the local Employment Exchange and that all salaried positions were advertised when vacancies occurred. There was also the added hitch that to be employed in the Corporation, you had to be a resident of the city for at least twelve months. In replying to a letter from his niece seeking work in the Corporation, the lord mayor counselled she would need to sit for the clerkships examinations.[255] Occasionally, replies from City Hall were

---

[254] Ibid.
[255] PRONI, LA/7/3/A/82.

accompanied by the rider, 'the lord mayor will keep your name before him'.[256]

Over the years, McCullagh's postbag contained letters of congratulation on his re-appointment as lord mayor. One such letter from the prime minister, John Andrews, having offered congratulations, expressed a hope for a happier relationship between the Corporation and the Government, with a plea that if the lord mayor foresaw any difficulties between the two bodies that he would come forward to 'talk matters over'. In response, the lord mayor assured the prime minister that he had always been anxious that good relations prevailed and that he would do everything in his power towards that end.[257] There were letters, too, from the Loyal Orange Lodges and the Masonic Lodge, showing McCullagh's close association with these bodies. These letters contained invitations to functions and records of the dues paid to them.[258]

## McCullagh on housing

Ever since his appointment as chairperson of the Corporation Housing Committee in 1919, and later in parliament, McCullagh expressed a passionate interest in housing the city's population. In pursuit of this endeavour, he didn't think government officials and civil servants were up to speed on the matter. He cavilled against parliament on their confused and mixed-up thinking surrounding the supply of new housing and the overcharging of rents. He considered

---

[256] PRONI, LA/7/3/A/43.
[257] PRONI, LA/7/3/A/115.
[258] PRONI, LA/7/3/A/69.

that one of the 'greatest evils' of the time was people with money buying up houses and then sub-letting them out as rooms or flats. McCullagh was critical of the money allocated to construct new parliamentary buildings at Stormont, with no concern about the city's housing problem.

McCullagh was adamant that the city's housing problem would only be solved when private enterprise was encouraged to build. This drive to involve private developers proved to be his weakness, leading to his downfall and a parliamentary inquiry finding fault with his too-close relationship with monied developers and estate agents, resulting in deficient and disorganised control of the Corporation finances.

During the 1920s, the Corporation spent £3 million on the reconstruction of Belfast with the development of improved roads and prioritising bridges. However, while McCullagh maintained that, unlike Dublin, there were no slums in the city, he conceded there were many streets with small houses; however, he insisted that any uninhabitable dwellings were taken down.

In both Belfast and Dublin, there was a massive housing problem in accommodating the city population in the years between the two World Wars. In 1926, the Megaw Enquiry blamed Belfast Corporation for corrupt administration in housing delivery and held McCullagh, chairman of the Housing Committee, responsible for the mess.

In Dublin, a similar corruption was alleged, and the Corporation went into administration in 1924 for six years. Alfie Byrne was not involved, but when he became lord mayor in 1930, there were unanswered questions about his involvement in the allocation of Corporation housing through his involvement with the Royal Liver Friendly Society.

The sorry condition of the Dublin city tenements had a worldwide reputation in the late 1920s and the new Corporation in 1930 set out to address the accommodation needs of the poorer classes. In its first year, they erected 2,000 new dwellings and during the 1930s endeavoured to build approximately 1,000 every year which was no mean achievement. In 1931, unemployed men were paid to clear derelict sites in anticipation of new housing initiatives.

The Depression of the 1930s hampered progress in house building. Byrne was now a senior trustee of the English-based Royal Liver Friendly Society and saw an excellent business opportunity for the Royal Liver to bankroll any new housing initiative. He helped to organise a loan of £35,000 for Bray Urban District Council, having already secured loans elsewhere for others through the good offices of Royal Liver. It is not clear what broker benefits Byrne may have accrued in the setting up of these loans, but in more recent times, his involvement as the lord mayor might be construed as a clear conflict of interest.

In the 1930s, when the Dublin Corporation initiated new public housing schemes in Crumlin, Drumcondra, and Marino, it was both a concern and an opportunity for Byrne. He had a vested interest in the rebuilding of the inner city, like developments in UK cities where tenements were demolished and new accommodation erected. A move to the outskirts risked depleting his constituency population.

An opportunity to keep his constituency population intact arose when he sat on the new housing committee of the reconstituted Corporation. He assertively lobbied officials on behalf of his constituents. His confidence and lobbying vigour grew when, in 1936, as a trustee of Royal Liver he brokered a deal between the Corporation and the company for a loan of £25,000. No conflict of interest was raised when it transpired that, in the matter of housing allocation, Royal Liver 'has the right of nominations of tenants'.[259]

In 1936, Dublin city's voting population doubled when the universal franchise was introduced. The rules of the system changed and in the new dispensation, 52% of the vote cast went to 28 candidates in the lord mayor's panel. It was a popular endorsement of the lord mayor himself.

However, a more damning indictment in the 1930s on how the lord mayor of Dublin 'sailed close to the wind' was Byrne's significant involvement in the newly founded Irish Hospital Sweepstakes, a lottery set up in 1930 with the purpose of funding hospital buildings in the country. Byrne had previous history in the lottery business. During the Great War, he joined forces with a bookmaker, Richard Duggan, to form a lottery that distributed funds to the family and crew of a merchant ship torpedoed off the coast of Wexford. That success led Byrne to organise the Harbour Sweep in 1920, which raised £100 for destitute children.

## Financial bedfellows

McCullagh's relationship with the Belfast businessman William Gibson and the Jew Otto Jaffé was key to his rise to prominence; and towards the end of the 1920s, he had also developed a close association and controversial dealings with the Jewish Berwitz brothers. McCullagh's association with the Jewish community in Belfast was probably not a casual

---

[259] White, p.118.

acquaintance but a shrewd understanding that 'the Jews had money and understood finance'. As Jewish businessmen came to represent the new face of money in society, money 'however recently acquired became an accepted means of entering it'.[260]

Byrne also had his mentors, but they were more transparent than McCullagh's and he was more open in acknowledging their influence. This was true for his association with the lottery business. When the opportunity to launch a new lottery came his way, Byrne embraced it with open arms. Since 1823, lotteries had been illegal, but the legislation governing them was more honoured in the breach than the practice. The Catholic Church favoured lotteries and sweepstakes to raise funds for beneficent purposes.[261] The Government in Independent Ireland in the 1920s disapproved of all lotteries because of the potential for fraud. The minister of Home Affairs, Kevin O'Higgins, thought it was impossible to eliminate fraud and corruption in the staging of sweepstakes.[262] He was not alone in thinking this as elsewhere they considered lotteries a menace to good government.[263]

In 1923, to evade the law, the bookmaker Richard Duggan moved his financial base to Switzerland and continued to organise his Irish lottery initiatives from there.[264] In the same year, Alfie Byrne, as acting lord mayor, 'a gregarious little man known to every Pat, Mike, and Joe in Dublin as "Alfie"',[265]

---

[260] S. Heffer, *The Age of Decadence: Britain 1880-1914* (London, 2017), p. 95.
[261] Marie Colman in IESH vol. xxix, 2002, p. 46.
[262] Ibid., p. 48.
[263] A. Webb, *The Clean Wweep* (London, 1968), p. 148.
[264] Colman, p. 45.
[265] Webb, p. 44.

supervised the lottery draw.

In 1930, a new Public Charitable Hospital's Act became law and plans were immediately underway to hold the first legal Irish Hospitals' Sweepstake. Richard Duggan, the 'mastermind of sweepstakes in the 1920s', was the go-to person to get things up and running and no sooner was Byrne ensconced in the Mansion House than his old pal approached him to help promote the new legal lottery.

Ever since the success of Duggan's first hospitals' sweepstake, the possibility of a more streamlined version had its merits. During the 1920s, Dublin's voluntary hospitals were in deep financial trouble, with their very existence threatened by the aftermath of wartime inflation. Furthermore, the volume of charitable endowments decreased as the Protestant backers took flight to England and elsewhere once the new Free State was set up.[266] The Government had little funds to redress the financial deficit.

The sweepstake idea was Dublin's opportunity, and the lord mayor, Alfie Byrne, was fully behind it. He arranged for the first launch to take place in the Mansion House. The demand for lottery tickets was phenomenal, and Byrne saw endless possibilities for aggrandisement. He became a ticket agent for the sweepstake with an office across the road from the Mansion House, and retained a man to sell the tickets.

The organisers of the lottery declared that the running costs would not go beyond nine percent of all contributions. Over time, that became a mythical aspiration, as most of the money raised was siphoned off elsewhere and little went to good causes. The historian of the Hospitals' Sweepstake

---

[266] Colman, p. 40.

wrote: 'To seek information [about] the system of distribution
. . . an impenetrable darkness covers all . . . every business has
its secrets, and the real secret of the Irish Sweep is how it
does its business at all.'[267]

In the early years, up to three-quarters of the sweepstake
tickets were sold in Britain until the authorities there saw fit
to stop the extraordinary flow of money out of the country
and introduced legislation to that effect. Byrne continued to
be a vigorous advocate of the lottery, as did other politicians
of the day who were bankrolled with funds that originated
from within the sweepstake itself.

Decades later, Byrne's biographer wrote: 'It is arguable
that the venture embodied some of the worst aspect of public
life in Ireland: the privatisation of what should be public
functions; the false veneer of charity; the corruption; and the
self-serving hypocrisy of the Church and the political
establishment... Alfie Byrne was among the earliest and
loudest champions of the gigantic wheeze'.[268]

Byrne was elected and returned to the Dáil in 1937 and the
following year he aspired to become president of Ireland but
failed to procure the political backing. Byrne's son later
related that the rebuff of his father's presidential bid 'was the
greatest disappointment of his father's career.[269] However,
there was consolation when the Corporation elected Byrne as
lord mayor of Dublin for the ninth time in 1938.

When the spectre of war loomed in the same year, Byrne
assured Dubliners that the Corporation 'would do everything
in its power to advance any plans for providing adequate air

---

[267] Webb, p. 162.
[268] White, p.65.
[269] Ibid., p.147.

raid precautions'.[270] When war broke out, Byrne weighed up his situation. There were indications that the role of lord mayor was beginning to pall for him. He conveyed to the *Irish Times* newspaper that the 'strain of the last year had been so great . . . that it had all affected his health'.[271] The position was playing heavily on his finances and his bank manager was concerned about the extent of his overdraft, which stood at €5,176. When rationing came in at the beginning of the war, he sold his car and bought a motorbike.

In June 1939, he stepped down as the lord mayor, but the aspiration to become lord mayor of Dublin did not evaporate in the years ahead. Ten years later, in 1949, Byrne ran for a tenth time to become lord mayor of the city. He received no encouragement from within the city council, and his son, Alfie Junior, was the sole vote in the council chamber in his favour. He ran again in 1951 and secured three votes.[272] He ran again in 1952 and 1953 without success. However, perseverance paid off in 1954 when, at seventy-two and after an absence of fifteen years, he once again became the lord mayor.

## Assessment

For thirty years, Alfie Byrne was a people's icon with popularity second to none. He served in the national parliaments of the United Kingdom and the Irish Free State, and he was the only person to serve as a member of parliament, a senator, a councillor, and to hold the office of

---

[270] *Irish Times*, 28 September 1938.
[271] *Irish Times*, 16 January 1939.
[272] White, p.179.

the lord mayor of Dublin at the same time.

He was a master promoter of his interests and his biographer concludes he was in ways a flawed icon, 'an absent father, fond of censorship, he crushed free speech when it suited him . . . the sort of politician who followed a mob *to pick up a few votes.'* He mixed in circles with shadowy figures, bookmakers enhancing his pocket through the sweepstakes and through his role in the Royal Liver organisation.[273]

Much has been made of Crawford McCullagh's alleged control of the Unionist-led Belfast City Council during the 1930s when he was lord mayor. When re-elected as lord mayor of Belfast in January 1931, after fifteen years away from the mayoral office, McCullagh's inaugural speech referred to the trade depression of the previous year and the heavy burden of rates and taxation in the city. He considered that it was the duty of the Corporation to keep their expenses as low as possible to help return prosperity to the city.

In a veiled reference to invidious acrimony among members of the council, he remarked that he had always felt that if council members expressed less suspicion of one another and displayed more sympathy towards each other, more could be achieved. He believed that no matter what political party or affiliation he represented, he had a commitment to a constituency of citizens to whom he was responsible and for whom he endeavoured to serve. If councillors bore this in mind, council deliberations would be more harmonious, and the honour and prestige of their beloved city would be enhanced. He would be fair to all

---

[273] Ibid., p.194.

parties and without bias.[274]

All through the 1930s, McCullagh worked hard in the Corporation to keep cohesion among the Unionist ranks. In December 1933, he became lord mayor for the seventh term which was then considered a record in the annals of the mayoralty of Belfast.[275] A baronetcy was conferred on McCullough in 1935 much to the delight of the city council who felt that they and the city had been indirectly honoured. In reply to the congratulations of council members, McCullagh referred to the support of his wife in terms of advice and assistance in promoting the welfare of Belfast citizens. He made mention of his son who also was of great assistance to him in his public duties.[276]

We could make an even stronger case of political aggrandisement for Alfie Byrne, who, as an independent political member in parliament, became a potent political power broker. Politics was everything to Byrne. It drove him like nothing else as he went about his daily business. When the Fianna Fáil party entered the Dáil in 1932, he hosted a meeting of prominent businessmen and citizens in the Mansion House in December 1932.

It was a significant meeting and the outcome months later saw the coming together of Cumann na nGaedheal, the National Centre Party, and the National Guard to form the new party of Fine Gael. However, before the new party could find its feet, De Valera, leader of Fianna Fáil, called a snap election and his party was returned to power.

Alfie Byrne was re-elected to his North City constituency.

[274] *Irish Times*, 24 January 1931.
[275] *Irish Times*, 16 December 1933.
[276] *Irish Times*, 4 January 1935.

In July 1955, Trinity College Dublin awarded him an honorary Doctorate of Law, with the citation that he 'held the office of lord mayor more frequently than any other man, whose name is linked all over the world with that of Dublin; a champion of the poor and needy, a friend of all men'.[277] In March 1976, while still a member of the Dáil and the Corporation, Byrne contracted pneumonia and died.

Alfie Byrne served ten years as lord mayor of Dublin. Crawford McCullagh served eighteen years as lord mayor of Belfast. Queens University Belfast never bestowed an honorary degree on McCullagh for services rendered to the city, though he received honours from the state during his time in parliament, the Senate, and for his work as lord mayor. Both Byrne and McCullagh flirted with questionable forces in the allocation of housing in their respective cities and were credited with organising cabals on their city councils. Today, the reputation of both men in the popular imagination is very different, with Sir Crawford McCullagh's legacy still open to interpretation.

---

[277] McEllin, 'Legendary Lord Mayor Alfie Byrne' in R. McManus and L. Griffith (eds), *Leaders of the City* (Dublin, 1913), p. 164.

# EPILOGUE

*Politics is almost as exciting as war, and quite as dangerous.*
*In war you can only be killed once, but in politics many times.*

Winston Churchill

*Every man has a rainy corner of his life,*
*whence comes foul weather which follows him.*

Jean Paul Richter

Ian Budge and Cornelius O'Leary in *Belfast: Approach to Crisis — a Study of Belfast Politics 1817-1970* make assertions about the Crawford McCullagh era in Belfast politics. They suggest that Crawford McCullagh, as lord mayor, exercised an 'extraordinary hold over the unionists on the Corporation' for a decade and a half and had a reputation for public and private hospitality that was legendary, not seen since the halcyon era of Belfast under the likes of Lord William Pirrie, Otto Jaffé and Shaftesbury.[278]

Budge and O'Leary attributed to him political savvy whereby 'the Unionist councillors established a permanent structure' that came to be known as the 'City Hall' party, with a leader, a secretary, a treasurer, and regular meetings. Yet, the evidence for this contention is less easy to ascertain. The senior archivist responsible for transferring the City Hall archive and files to the Public Record Office of Northern Ireland found no evidential material that would support the theory that there was a concerted and organized Unionist

---

[278] I. Budge and C. O'Leary, *Belfast: Approach to Crisis* (London, 1973), p. 155.

party machine in City Hall. Certainly, the Unionist headquarters in Glengall Street harboured no archive on a 'City Hall' Unionist party.[279]

If there are problems sourcing a City Hall archive that confirm McCullagh at the fulcrum of Unionist power, there is even less possibility that he exercised power of any kind when he was a member of the first Northern Ireland parliament. Furthermore, there are unanswered questions about his chairing of a City Hall housing committee in the 1920s when committee members lined their pockets without his knowledge – or was he just too naïve a chairperson to comprehend what was going on around him?

When the Whiteabbey crisis arose in 1941, McCullagh's failed leadership on the city council inevitably led to the Corporation going into administration at the behest of the Government. Rather than harbour the belief that McCullagh has somehow been written out of history, as suggested by his biographer and others, maybe he played a very minor role in the orchestration of City Hall affairs.

On one level, his ubiquitous sitting on this or that committee in the Corporation, and in the first Belfast parliament, is impressive, yet a lasting contribution to matters of importance is hard to quantify. He was undoubtedly a staunch Unionist and the Prime Minister, Lord Brookeborough, confirmed this in a glowing tribute to him when he retired as lord mayor.

As lord mayor, he was always in the public eye and refused few opportunities to attend meetings, dinners and gala entertainment. Consequently, the four-volume archival

---

[279] I. Montgomery, PRONI archivist, in conversation with the author.

material on Crawford McCullagh, deposited in the Linen Hall Library, reads more like a tabloid pictorial rather than revealing a politician of substance. Emulating the great Lord Pirrie, he never took money from the public purse to lavishly entertain visiting guests and dignitaries when they visited City Hall. Pirrie's time as lord mayor was short-term compared to McCullagh's eighteen years, but Pirrie ended up bankrupt, something that a coterie of colleagues miraculously kept hidden from his family and wife.

How McCullagh rose from modest beginnings to become a wealthy magnate in Belfast in late Victorian and Edwardian times is still somewhat of a mystery. Was his wealth individually mined or was he a convenient and willing conduit for the money and investments of other city barons in a Belfast that mirrored the new emerging cities in America at the time?

His first sojourn as lord mayor was during the Great War and, in 1931, he was again elected as lord mayor and kept that office until 1946 while serving in the Northern Ireland Senate. In his ninth year as lord mayor, McCullagh was feted for his 'outstanding ability' with which he had discharged his onerous responsibilities and the strict impartiality which marked his reign in office. He was involved in prolonged negotiations in connection with the new site for the Boyne Bridge and the success of the new venture led for a call to organise an exhibition to promote the industries of Belfast around the United Kingdom, with the portrayal of the city as having the largest shipbuilding yard, the largest rope works, the largest tobacco factory and largest linen industry in the world.[280]

---

[280] *Irish Times*, 19 December 1936.

In1938, he had been lord mayor of the city eleven times and had held the mayoral chair consecutively for the previous eight years. The minority Nationalist members of the Corporation paid tribute to him, noting that he 'had been kind and considerate to the most humble member of the council, and if he had erred, it had been in leniency to the minority in the City Council'.[281]

McCullagh's obituary pays tribute to a man who served his community with generosity, largesse and commitment, exercising a pivotal role in local government.[282] He was a powerful figure in the political interplay between the new Northern Ireland administration and Belfast Corporation – a fact that grudgingly drew from the prime minister, James Craig, the recognition that 'we always have to bear in mind that the city represents in many respects one-half of Northern Ireland and therefore requires careful handling'.[283]

When the newly elected John Andrews succeeded Craig as prime minister, he wrote a letter to McCullagh expressing his concern that good relations would prevail between the Corporation and the Government. McCullagh in his reply assured him he personally would do all in his power to bring this about.[284]

There was a growing sense that the Corporation itself throughout the 1930s was out of its time in understanding how it should govern. The new state of Northern Ireland from its inception experienced enormous problems of finance and a dogged political apathy. Before partition,

---

[281] *Irish Times*, 15 December 1938.
[282] *Belfast Newsletter*, 14 April 1948.
[283] P. Buckland, *Factory of Grievances* (Dublin, 1979), p. 40.
[284] PRONI, LA/7/3A/115.

Dublin Castle rather than local authorities took the enterprising initiatives and responsibility for how money was spent at the local level. After the setting up of the Northern Ireland state, there was a mindset that continued to expect that the central Government, now the provincial parliament, would pick up the tab for most costs.

In this respect, Belfast Corporation became a thorn in the side of the new administration, and when they underachieved, they blamed the Government for their own ineptitude and lethargy. This proved essentially counterproductive, as it only reinforced the view that the Corporation was, in the words of Patrick Buckland, 'ill-equipped . . . to run the affairs of a modern city'.[285]

Belfast Corporation had three pivotal areas of responsibility – housing, health and education and, during his time there, Crawford McCullagh was mainly associated with housing. House building in Belfast had come to a virtual standstill during the First World War. The Local Government (Ireland) Act 1919 required the Corporation to draw up its housing scheme and Crawford McCullough became chairman of a fourteen-man Housing Committee. The scheme became notorious for corrupt practice and in the ensuing parliamentary Commission of Inquiry, Robert Megaw identified McCullagh as the 'greatest factor' in the actions undertaken by the Housing Committee.

The Megaw Inquiry identified McCullagh as 'the actual as well as the nominal leader of the Committee throughout its existence. He put the Committee in possession of such information as it had when the policy was to be formulated or

---

285 P. Buckland, p. 166.

approved. He brought the decision of the Committee before the City Council, in which he evidently had great weight and authority'.[286]

In the aftermath of the report, the city solicitor and surveyor had to resign, and persons implicated in housing contracts were prosecuted. Sir Crawford McCullagh miraculously survived, but he was undoubtedly tainted. In 1929, he lost his seat in the Cromac district of the Corporation.[287] He bounced back and was elected for the Woodvale District in1930, and the Corporation's General Purposes Committee rallied around and chose him as the next lord mayor of Belfast. He held office for the next sixteen years, with a brief break in 1942.

Budge and O'Leary suggest that McCullagh's hold on the Unionist-dominated Corporation throughout the inter-war period was his extreme hospitality, and that it played a significant part in his influence. He was a wealthy man, and he enjoyed spreading his wealth around.[288] Others feared that his patronage had a debilitating influence on the body politic. The historian of Ulster and Belfast, Jonathon Bardon, wrote that McCullagh possessed 'great charm, and enormous energy and devotion to political life'. His Unionist friends saw him as 'an ideal ambassador for the city, not least because his hospitality was lavish and he funded civic entertainment out of his own pocket'.[289] While there was prestige associated with mayoralty, the apparent need for deep pockets kept many a would-be lord mayor at bay.

---

[286] The Megaw Enquiry (1926), p. 117.
[287] *Belfast Newsletter*, 16 January 1929.
[288] *Belfast Newsletter*, 14 April 1948.
[289] F. W. Boal and S.A. Royal, *Enduring City* (Belfast, 2006), p. 128.

Again, a more fundamental consideration might be that the probable source of McCullagh's supposed dominance on the Corporation lay in the fact that during the 1930s, Unionist councillors as a group developed a semi-permanent structure that became a successful mechanism for Unionists to monopolise and control all office appointments within the Corporation. The so-called 'City Hall party' was anathema to Unionist headquarters in Glengall Street, and the elections in 1936 demonstrated clear disagreement between them over two candidates standing for the Clifton district.

A lesser-known and never commented upon aspect of the source of McCullagh's control in the Corporation was his lifelong association with the masonic lodges that offered an aura of secrecy, bonding men who played a role in business and public life in the city. City Hall files record the lodgement of membership fees to masonic lodges in the lord mayor's papers.[290]

Freemasonry is today viewed more benignly than it was back in the 1930s. Modern society better understands freemasonry not to be a secret society but a society with a few secrets, mainly concerned with modes of mutual recognition. In the early twentieth century, the main churches outlawed freemasonry because of the closed nature of their membership practices and the perception of how their modus operandi impinged on society at large.

In 1917, the Code of Canon Law (Canon 2335) in the Catholic church named masonic groups as forbidden societies with the threat of ex-communication for those who became involved. The main Protestant churches found offence in the

---

[290] PRONI, LA/7/3A/69.

allegations of masons dabbling in mysticism, occultism and possible Satanism. Many Christian men, discouraged by their church from joining the Freemasons, opted to join similar fraternal organisations like the Knights of Columbanus or the Orange Order. McCullagh was a member of the Orange Order *and* a freemason.

While McCullagh was at the centre of a disciplined party machine in the Corporation, there are substantial references to strategy meetings and cabals recorded in the Corporation minutes that verify the existence of a Unionist elite in the council. In 1926, Megaw declared McCullagh carried 'great weight and authority' in that body. Under his chairmanship during the inter-war period, there were several constructive developments – a new airport and the resurfacing of city streets. In 1938, McCullagh negotiated with Earl of Shaftesbury for the donation of Belfast Castle and its demesne of 200 acres to the city. He also opened the Floral Hall. The success of the Belfast gasworks as a commercial concern was a particular source of pride to McCullagh. While the Corporation had to import coal, McCullagh boasted that gas was supplied cheaper to the citizens of Belfast than in any other place in the United Kingdom.[291]

When war broke out in 1939, the Belfast Corporation was deficient in matters of civic defence, particularly in the provision of air raid shelters. Yet, the record shows that this was not a failure on McCullagh's part. During that first year of the war, he consistently argued for the erection of air raid shelters. He did not agree with people who said there was little chance of an air raid on Belfast by the Germans and he

---

[291] H.C. Deb. (N.I.), 3, c. 218.

actually named the people who said there would be no war: they were the very people 'who now tell us there was no need for shelters'.[292] Yet he wasn't able to convince fellow councillors to do something about erecting shelters. Then, councillors further rejected his recommendations for reform arising from the Dunlop Report on the Whiteabbey affair in 1941 – power was ebbing away both from McCullagh and the Corporation itself.

Corporation members of longstanding and dedicated service had made their contribution, and it was now time for a change. McCullagh stepped down as lord mayor, but when the incoming mayor suddenly died, McCullagh was re-elected. The Government saw the need to seize the day and clip the wings of a recalcitrant Corporation and they put it into administration for three and a half years while McCullagh remained on as a titular leader until 1946.

McCullagh, over his lifetime in business and politics, unlike the proverbial prophet, had indeed received honours in his own time and his own place. From 1906, he was elected first to the Cromac district, then to Woodvale district. He was High Sheriff of Belfast in 1911 and elected Lord Mayor of Belfast in 1914, 1915 and 1916. He received a knighthood in 1915 and made a freeman of the City of Belfast in 1917. He was elected to the first Northern Ireland parliament in 1921 and he lord mayor of Belfast from 1931 until 1946 (with a slight gap in 1942).

He was a member of the Northern Ireland Senate for fifteen years, became a baronet in 1935 and a sworn member of the Privy Council of Northern Ireland in 1942. When he

---

[292] H.C. Senate Deb. (N.I.), 22, c. 340.

was re-elected as lord mayor in 1935, the prime minister, Lord Craigavon, wrote him a personal handwritten letter of congratulations: 'It is with very special pleasure that, on the one hand, I congratulate you on your re-election as Lord Mayor for the eight time, and on the other, thank you again for shouldering the heavy burden of responsibility . . . I can only add that I feel quite sure that the Council have done the right thing. Yours sincerely, Craigavon'.[293] In modern times, the refurbished City Hall paid the ultimate long-term tribute to Sir Crawford McCullagh and his wife with two magnificent stained-glass windows at the top of the main stairway in the building.

Yet, even today, the jury is still out on who Crawford McCullagh was and how significant his contribution to Belfast civic life was. Was he a louche businessman of his time? Was he a Unionist boss who controlled how the party operated on Belfast Corporation? McCullagh's interview with the press when he retired from full-time business in 1928 was revealing. He claimed then that he had no interest in making money, but his energy and raison d'être came via the buzz that life in commerce afforded. However, one does not accumulate wealth without a capacity for the detail required in the practical pursuit of trade and industry. It may well be true that McCullagh had no head for detail in his business dealings and that it was others around him who had the business acumen that allowed him to claim that he was a self-made businessman.

His lack of a 'head for detail' frustrated the Megaw Inquiry over the corruption in the housing committee from 1925 to

---

[293] PRONI, LA/7/3A/38.

26. Time and time again, when questioned, McCullagh showed a blatant lack of recollection of relevant matters. Megaw was further frustrated when McCullagh's deputy chairperson was deliberately kept away from the inquiry when his presence would have compensated for McCullagh's loss of memory. Again, in the Whiteabbey affair in 1941, McCullagh, as lord mayor and leader of the council, didn't appear to have any grasp initially of what was awry in the hospital's administration.

Perhaps the one true failure in Crawford McCullagh's time on Belfast Corporation, after the First World War, was the pressure exercised on the Government by the Corporation members to remove proportional representation as the method of election for local authorities. In a historian's view, 'the move killed political life in Belfast more effectively even than elaborate gerrymandering did in Derry'.[294] McCullagh was entirely in favour of the removal of proportional representation and spoke to that effect in parliament.[295] The Local Government Act (1922) saw the abolition of PR and it guaranteed that Unionist dominance on the Corporation was assured. Belfast Corporation, under Sir Crawford McCullagh's leadership during the inter-war period, had a poor record of social reform. It had marked time and mirrored the politics of a century earlier when the control of all offices by one party helped to embed the 'ancient and festering tradition of municipal corruption'.

---

[294] K. Johnson, *In the Shadows of Giants* (Dublin, 2008), p. 238.
[295] H. C. Deb. (N.I.), 2, c. 638.

# ABOUT THE AUTHOR

Austin Stewart is a former history teacher and founder member of the Maynooth University History Forum. His monograph, *Coalisland, County Tyrone, in the Industrial Revolution, 1800-1901,* in the Maynooth University history series, remains a pioneering assessment of the impact of industrialisation in a mid-Ulster town in the nineteenth century.

Printed in Great Britain
by Amazon

84277034R00112